Not Like My Mother

Becoming a sane parent after growing up in a CRAZY family

by

Irene Tomkinson, MSW

authorHOUSE®

AuthorHouse™
1663 Liberty Drive, Suite 200
Bloomington, IN 47403
www.authorhouse.com
Phone: 1-800-839-8640

This book is a work of non-fiction. Unless otherwise noted, the author
and the publisher make no explicit guarantees as to the accuracy of
the information contained in this book and in some cases, names of
people and places have been altered to protect their privacy.

First published by AuthorHouse 2/11/2008

ISBN: 978-1-4343-2263-0 (sc)

Library of Congress Control Number: 2007909016

Printed in the United States of America
Bloomington, Indiana

This book is printed on acid-free paper.

Cover design by David Random, www.davidrandom.com

Cover photo by Shawn Tomkinson, www.shawntphoto.com

Dedication

To my Mom and John…for all of their love…
To my sisters, Dorothy and Jackie…for all of our history…
To my sister-of-the-heart, Bev…for all of her trust…
To my daughters, Lynn and Shawn for being my greatest teachers…
To my first grandchild, Julia…for showing me the future…
And most importantly to my husband, David…
for all of our "Harvest Moons"

From my Essence,
Me

In Gratitude

Writing this gratitude page has been one of the most difficult parts of the whole writing process. I know I have not been able to remember everyone who held out a hand to me along this journey. Please know that my heart remembers even if this 61-year-old brain of mine can't. I was naive when I began this book. I had no idea how long the process would take and how many people would generously give me their time, support, encouragement, wisdom and even money.

How do I thank my wonderful circle of friends and family, my earth angels, who held my dream for me until I could hold it for myself – until it was a reality?

I thank each of you with a heart filled with awe and wonder...

a heart flowing with gratitude and

a heart flying with hope.

To each of you I say …Namaste.

Special Appreciation and Acknowledgement to

Nancy Eichhorn - Everett Moitoza – Elizabeth Hall-Moitoza - Carrie Carr -Beth Gilmore –William Gilmore - David Random

With deep gratitude to

Nancy Aronie	P.J. Campbell
Dan Brown	Dot Farnsworth
Diane Cirincione	Lauren Hidden
Karen Fitzgerald	Barbara Knapp
Gerry G. Jampolsky, M.D	Linda Parker
Jennifer Michaud	Kate Portrie
Marty Random	Sareen Sarna
Judith Ryan	Tom Stubbs
Leslie Smith	Donna Witham
Jackie Watson	

and of course the "Snerdettes"

Contents

SECTION TWO: UNDERSTANDING OUR-SELVES

SECTION THREE: DEVELOPING HEALTHY RELATIONSHIPS

Preface

I wrote this book to give you freedom. I want you to have freedom from the grip of your crazy or painful childhood. I found freedom for myself. I have helped others find it. And now I want you to have it.

This book is my journey of identifying, healing, and moving on from the legacy of a crazy family.

It is my story of being raised in a crazy family. Then it is my story of becoming a crazy parent. And finally, it is my story of breaking the cycle.

As a mom I struggled in my relationships with my daughters; as a therapist, I have had the opportunity to see my own story reflected back to me in many of the lives of my clients. A graduate school research project launched me into finding a path out of the generational craziness that was my legacy.

I share with you the healing that I have experienced. I want you to know the healing that is possible for you and your family. I want to help you to stop family craziness for the next generation.

Were you like me? Did you promise that you would be a different kind of parent than your mom and dad? I'll show you how those promises are actually keeping you stuck in your painful childhood. Are you feeling disappointment and frustration with yourself as well as with your own kids? I've been there, too. I'll help you see how your childhood experiences are feeding your frustrations, how your parents' childhood impacted the way they parented you and how your childhood impacts the way you parent your children.

You will recognize how the behaviors you used as a kid to keep yourself safe and sane are the same behaviors that are blocking your relationships today. Because your family environment, for whatever reason, was not able to meet your needs, you were left with a void—an injury. That injury needs to be healed.

In this book, we are going to look at our relationships with our children. But as you will see, all of our relationships have been impacted by our crazy childhoods. Most importantly, our childhood has shaped our relationship with *ourselves.*

You were drawn to the title of this book for a reason. You are reading this preface for a reason. Know that when the student is ready, the teacher appears. You are ready, that is why you picked up my book. Let ***Not Like My Mother*** be your teacher.

Blessings,

Irene Tomkinson, MSW

February 18, 2007

SECTION ONE
MY STORY

Chapter 1:

Parenting—When Is the Job Done?

Our Christmas letter would have looked like a script for the Jerry Springer show!

I was 51 years old and in my last year of graduate school. As a final research project, my professor suggested to the class that we research a question that personally challenged us. "What are you always asking yourself?" he queried. My silent response was immediate: *Parenting— when is the job done?* Just as automatic was my answer . . . *never!* At the time my daughters were 31 and 32.

I thought I was joking. But the more I examined the question, the more I knew I was serious. I wanted the answer. Ok. I didn't expect the "job" to be done. But when would it be easy or fun again? Why had parenting become such a frustrating experience for me? It was fun when the girls were young. I did feel successful then. However, after they reached adolescence, all bets were off. What happened? I used to be their hero. Now we had difficulty being in the same car for a trip to the mall.

I was a woman who knew success. I was confident in a variety of areas of my life, both professional and personal. Yet, in my relationships with my daughters, I seldom felt competent. The one thing in life I wanted to do perfectly, I feared I was ultimately blowing. Maybe I hadn't completely blown it, but I never arrived at any sustained sense of "*Yes, Irene—job well done!*"

I continually saw any pain or struggle experienced by my daughters, Lynn and Shawn Mary, as evidence of my failure. I felt frustration and guilt. I was convinced that if I had done my job right, they would be happy.

I easily became frustrated and irritated with each of them and they with me. Somewhere between playing with LEGOs and blowing out their thirteen birthday candles, we went from "Mommy, I'm never going to leave you," to "Mom, I can't wait to move out and never have to listen to you again." I often had a hard time hearing them because I was screaming something loving like, "Puhleeze let me help you pack!"

I was sick and tired of the dance we danced. How was this happening? I aggravated them the way my mom aggravated me. They hated my "nagging" the way I hated *my* mom's "preaching." And I was seeing their choices as clearly self-destructive and self-sabotaging. If they used their heads, I would not have to lose my temper. I could sleep at night. Whenever they were faced with a life challenge and I felt they made a poor choice, I would turn the situation into "I didn't do the mother job right"! I had worked so hard for things to be different from *my* adolescence. And now they are adults and we are still fighting. How could it be going so wrong, so often, and for so long?

Sometimes I secretly wondered if the frustration and disappointment I felt meant I didn't love my daughters. I didn't buy that. Sure I wanted to kill them, but hey, I always loved them. I loved their talents and intelligence. I loved their creativity and sense of humor. I loved their hearts, each different, yet each beautiful. I respected their honesty and their wonderful sense of adventure.

I just yearned to be free from judgment and friction. I didn't want any more conflict. I wanted to be lovingly detached…not be so involved or easily upset. My mothering needed a tad more Mother Theresa and a lot less Lizzy Borden. I also did not want one more argument with my husband about the girls or my interactions with them. There had to be a better way than the way our family was communicating. I wanted the damn manual. Please God, let me stop being jealous of anyone who chose not to have children. The bad news was my desperation. The good news was the willingness and motivation my desperation gave me. I would do whatever I needed to do. I wanted to know what other parents were doing right. What did they know that I didn't?

So who knew? Who could tell me what sane relationships between parents and grown children should look like and how could I learn to bring some of that health into my family?

For years I hated Christmas letters. The truth is I hated and liked them at the same time. I liked catching up on the lives of friends I might only hear from once a year. What I hated was the contrast I noted between the perfect lives portrayed in those letters and the way my family was trudging along.

I read those photocopied holiday letters as if they were job performance reviews from the successful parents. They were the parents who were doing the job right! I figured the folks who sent those letters were making a public announcement on snowflake-trimmed paper that they were in the "good parents club." Yearly they listed their offspring's accomplishments in print. Their kids finished high school with awards and scholarships, graduated college in four years, acquired high paying jobs with good benefits, and, of course, were involved in meaningful volunteer work. (What, no cures for cancer? No one nominated for a Nobel Peace Prize?) From where I sat, those letters arrived like an annual indictment clearly stating—*Irene, you didn't do it right.*

Meanwhile, back at our house, my girls had struggled with adolescent rebellion and substance abuse. They dropped in and out and back into college. And like many of their peers, they found it difficult to make ends meet financially.

As a family, poor communication skills and a demanding genetic pool challenged us all. Alcoholism and its many DNA cousins reached back in my family and my ex-husband, Kevin's family as far as the twinkle in our blarney-filled Irish eyes could see. If I had sent a family Christmas letter, it would have looked like a script for *The Jerry Springer Show.*

What did these Christmas-letter-parents know that I didn't? I had all the best intentions. I wanted as much for my kids as anyone else. What were my second husband, David and I doing wrong? How come we were sooo *not a* Christmas-letter-family? What was missing? Those damn letters were the final push. I was going to find a better way.

I was on a mission. My plan was to use my graduate school research project as an excuse to interview 100 parents with grown children between the ages of 16-85 plus. It all seemed quite simple to me. I would ask each of the 100 parents to share with me what they thought worked well in their relationships with their grown children. Basically, I was collecting how-to recipes for getting along with your grown kids.

I figured by the end of the semester I would not only have finished the class requirement but, as an added bonus, I would have unlocked the secrets of the "good parents." I likened it to when Lynn and Shawn Mary were little and I went to Dr. Benjamin Spock's book for answers. I was excited to begin.

I was ready to record the great gems, pass my project with flying colors, and, best of all, have a workable game plan for my own family.

Well, as most things in life go, it wasn't that simple. I asked, but these parents didn't know. Over and over again, parents would answer my inquiry with, "Hmmmm, what works well in my relationship with my kids? I could better tell you what *doesn't work*." Few could tell me what worked and those that tried were vague. Many of the people I interviewed felt the same sense of disappointment I felt. In a matter of minutes, parents opened up as if they had been waiting with heavy luggage for a shuttle bus or porter. They were looking for some relief from their burden. They very much needed to unload. I was surprised, and truth be told—validated. They felt much like I did.

People shared painful family arguments that had left tension and wounds between themselves and their children. They shared how they worried about their grown children's choices and lifestyles. These parents fretted over what they could do to help. Others described tiptoeing around their kids so as not to rock the relationship boat. Parents talked about money issues they had with their kids and how often that led to arguments with their spouses—"You give the kids too much money," or "When do we say no?" or "Why are you so cheap?" or "We need to help them." It went on and on.

Many of these volunteer research participants complained that their kids only called when they wanted something. They also struggled with their kids' lifestyles and the way grandchildren were being raised. They unanimously felt some responsibility for any pain or unhappiness they perceived their adult children were experiencing. And everyone at some time or another felt guilt for the way they had parented. No one described easy, flowing, comfortable relationships with their kids.

What was going on? This couldn't be the story for everyone. I was sure someone somewhere was having an easy go of it. Someone must be enjoying the ride. Who was writing those Christmas letters?

Then it happened. While reading Steven Covey's book, *Seven Habits of Highly Effective Families*, a light went on that illuminated my dilemma. Steven referred to his childhood and how much he had wanted to give his own children the same experience he had growing up. He admired and wanted to emulate his mom and dad. Some of his frustrations were with the state of the world and how it differs from when he was a boy. He felt it was much more challenging, given today's world, to be an effective parent. He believed that his parents lived in an easier time.

There it was! Bingo! Double whammy! I lived in the same turbulent time as Steven, but I did not have a good model for parenting. So that was how he got the instruction manual! His parents gave it to him. I did not want to parent the way I was parented. I wanted just the opposite of what I experienced as a child. I parented from a determination that my daughters would *not* have the same family experience I had.

If you are like Steven Covey, *pleased with the way you were raised by your parents,* you modeled your parenting after your own childhood experience. (And you are probably not reading this book.)

On the other hand, if you did not agree with the way you were parented, if you felt that your parents didn't meet your needs as a kid, then you either committed to not having children or to parent the opposite of your parents. Your reference point for parenting was your own childhood, your history. Your eyes were on the past. This is not a bad thing if the past gives you a good example. But if your past was filled with the hurt and pain of unmet childhood needs and you were determined to "do it differently," then therein lies the problem— *knowing what you don't want to do was not a plan and still isn't.*

Can you imagine trying to build a house and the only instructions you have for the contractor is a list of what you don't want? The list may offer a bit of help but certainly is incomplete at best. And, ladies and gentlemen, that was my parenting agenda in a nutshell. I wanted my kids to have a completely different childhood experience than I had. I did not want their family experience to be like mine. I was well-versed in *what I did not want for my kids.*

Interviewing parents further showed me I was not alone. The majority of parents I spoke with felt the same way. (Note: Many of the people I used in my research project readily identified themselves as growing up in family environments that they described as crazy or dysfunctional). You grew up in a crazy family if you had a family environment that did not feel safe; a family that, for whatever reason, was not able to give you the physical or emotional support that you needed to thrive and flourish.

I didn't write this book to convince you that you did or didn't grow up in a crazy family. But if you identify with the idea of growing up in a crazy family, a family that was not able to meet your needs as a kid, then know it or not, you have an agenda you are looking for your kids to fulfill. The voids left from our unmet childhood needs set impossible unspoken agendas for us as adults. These old wounds continue to hold us hostage and make many decisions for us in all our relationships without our acknowledgement or permission. This phenomenon is particularly true as we parent.

When our kids don't fulfill our agendas (and they won't because it is an impossible task, and also it is not their job), then we feel incomplete, frustrated, and inadequate. We know something is wrong. We can't define it. In the meantime, we make do. We try to live with it. We wiggle and squirm in it. But we don't know what the *it* is. Is it us? Is it them? We say things we don't want to say. We react and spin dramas and crises reminiscent of our own childhoods while the circumstances appear completely different.

We swing from blaming our kids for the craziness, to ourselves, to God, to sugarcoated cereals and the damn television. All the while our relentless self-critic convinces us we aren't doing the parenting job right. Many of us figured it was just a matter of doing the job differently than our parents. But we can't do anything from what we *don't* want. We can't order dinner in a restaurant, we can't buy clothes, we can't find friends, we can't build a house, we can't move forward. What we *don't want* is not a plan. It is not a blueprint or a model. It is a setup for staying stuck in our history. It keeps us focused on our past. It keeps us stalled in the childhood we wanted to escape.

Through my research, my workshops, and, of course, by making lots of mistakes with my kids, I have learned the importance of separating "my childhood story" from my parenting. It is in our childhoods where our "crazy" agendas are set. I didn't know I had an agenda left over from my childhood that I was looking for my kids to fulfill. I sincerely thought I wanted them to be or do anything they could possibly imagine. If that were true, then what agenda did I have for them?

To acknowledge the agenda I had for my kids, I needed to meet my own story. I had to collect my own history. I could not just cut back the dead overgrowth. I had to dig up the roots and turn the soil. Until we own our history, until we recognize how our childhood experience landed on us, we cannot know ourselves. We can't know what we did with our experiences; we cannot be present to effectively participate in any of our relationships, especially our relationships with our children.

I had enough frustration and pain to make me willing to learn whatever I needed to learn, in order that I might understand what I was doing wrong. Eventually, the "Idea Angels" got through my thick defenses. When the student is ready, the teacher appears. I became the student, and teachers in many forms did indeed appear. My research had boiled down to a case study and I was the patient.

I did answer the question, "Parenting—when is the job done?" But more than *when*, I answered the question—*how*. This book is the answer. With the help and trust of many wonderful and courageous workshop participants, clients, family, friends, twelve-step recovery programs, and the grace of the healing energy of the Universe, I found a path for healing. I found a path for confidence. I am no longer up to my ankles in the mud of insecurity. I am standing on dry, solid ground in my relationships with each of my grown daughters and their spouses. David (who adopted Lynn and Shawn Mary when they were 6 and 7) and I are no longer arguing about my interactions with the girls. Along the way, the process graced me with the bonus and blessing of a permanent healing of my own childhood wounds.

I didn't find the cure for aging or the quick way to miracle weight loss. What I found was a way out of my history and into the present. The journey took me from my head—through my fear—to my heart. As Anne Lamott in her book *Plan B* says, "It is not a journey of descent but a journey of ascent." On the way, I cleared a lot of dead brush and weeds, making a clearing that has opened up room for *me.*

My parenting future has been opened wide to the light of today. I am now able to take up space in my own life as never before. I have found peace. I will always be my daughters' mother. What has changed is that I am a mother I like being, no longer a mother in yesterday, but rather a mother in today. Not the mother I needed, I am the mother they need. Along the way, I found me.

Authors' Note

I have put a question at the end of each chapter for you to contemplate. Good therapists, like good consultants, don't have the right answers—they have the right questions. You have your own answers. You only need to be willing to sit with the questions.

Questions that are the most uncomfortable for us to sit with are usually questions that are forcing us to step out of our comfort zone. Human beings dislike change. We will go towards what is familiar before we will go towards joy.

A question for reflection . . .

How much pain do you need before you will change?

If you are inclined, write about it.

A recommendation:

Write on unlined paper because, without limitations, much more will be revealed to you.

Chapter 2:

How A Family Gets To Be Crazy?

People run away from their painful feelings.

So here is how my story began. I'll give you the short version because it is the only version I know. Should I start by saying once upon a time?

My father, James Joseph Smith, was sent to Sing Sing prison in Ossining, New York at the age of 16 for some petty teenage crime. In 1922, kids were not separated from the adult inmate population. While serving his time, he was raped. He murdered the man who raped him, and for that offense, fifteen more years were added to his sentence.

Mary Diaz, my mom, was born in New Bedford, Massachusetts in 1919. When Mom was eight years old, her mother died of tuberculosis. Shortly after the death of my grandmother, Mom was sexually abused by a day laborer who worked in my grandfather's bakery. My grandfather, filled with the pain of losing his wife and my mother's abuse, turned his feelings into a blistering hate for America. He then packed up his business, his home, my mother, and her baby sister and moved his life back to Portugal, his homeland. The year was 1930.

My grandfather was a man who spoke with his fists and punctuated his communication with the belt from his pants. My grandfather was

11

also a man who lived by the rules of his Portuguese father. He owned his land, his home, his hired help, and his children. They would do as he said or pay the consequences. He saw no practical use for women to be educated. Motivated by rage-filled determination, Mom held on tight to her goal of returning to her birthplace. Fourteen years after leaving America, she made her way back to what she calls, "My United States."

In 1944, at age 25, disowned by her father, Mom arrived in New York City by boat from Lisbon. World War II was coming to an end. My father, fresh from prison and mother, just off the boat from Lisbon, met while working in the garment industry of Manhattan. They helped to manufacture teddy bears.

I call it date rape. Mom says, "Your father forced himself on me." Whatever the circumstances, I came nine months later. They married in August in a civil ceremony at the city hall of Yonkers, New York. I was born in November. Mom was so filled with shame that she later had her picture taken in a white wedding gown by a professional photographer. I always wondered why there was only that one professional picture of her wedding and no pictures of the cake or guests or my father. She said the other pictures were destroyed in a basement flood. I was in my early thirties when she shared the truth.

Their union produced one more child—my younger sister, Dorothy. My father numbed his feelings, his pain, with compulsive gambling, and Mom looked for relief in another relationship. By the time I was three years old, my parents separated. Mom moved Dotty and me to Glen Burnie, Maryland and into her next marriage. We never saw our father again.

Throughout her life, Mom chased her childhood dream of having a picture perfect family. She imagined a faithful, loving husband by her side, a pretty house with a picket fence, and family always present. She could not tolerate being alone. She often said, "My fear of loneliness is like a disease." Mom's *loneliness* was a hole; a void left by the death of my grandmother. Mom's fear of emotional pain kept her from ever completing the grieving process. She didn't allow herself to feel (and thus identify and finish) the emotional pain she suffered as a child when her mother died.

Without embracing her childhood emotional pain, Mom had no information to allow her to unlock the wounded little girl trapped inside of her own heart. Without acknowledgment of her painful feelings, Mom was not able to give herself the compassion she deserved. Consequently, her grief was never finished. Mom just dragged it around for her entire life. Instead of owning and releasing her painful feelings, she buried the pain alive in a back drawer of her subconscious.

The intense longing for the connection and family she never had as a child, blinded her to reality. She chased her dream through six husbands: Manuel, James, Tony, Jack, Stewart, and John; through five states, and through numerous addresses until she ran smack into the middle of Alzheimer's disease, where she still resides today.

This quote from Karen Casey's book, *Each Day A New Beginning*, puts it all in a sentence—"The only pain we can avoid is the pain we get into trying to avoid pain."

My name, Irene, was my maternal grandmother's name. If Mom couldn't have her mother, at least she could have me. Mother never recognized what responsibility she handed me when she had me christened as Irene. She thought she was honoring her mother.

Mom was not able to see what burden she placed on me because she was too wrapped up in surviving. From childhood, she had insulated herself in an effort to survive the pain of her mom's death. She built her defense systems, as we all do, to ward off her original emotional pain. She had no understanding of the price she and others paid for the numbing. She was much too afraid to do any digging and to find out.

Unfortunately, our culture views numbing difficult feelings as a sign of strength. We believe surviving means our pain must be shut out. Our mental health medical system is based on containing and numbing feelings. We have an entire pharmaceutical industry built on keeping us away from pain—physical, as well as emotional. To disconnect from our hurtful feelings, we must disconnect from our bodies. We have to live in our heads. Whatever we use, be it fantasy or drugs, food or gambling, work or relationship addiction; when we are living from our heads and out of our bodies, we are separated from our *knowing,* from our *intuition,* and from our *wisdom.*

We fear that if we allow ourselves to feel our pain, "to go there"—we will die. It will "kill us." We are convinced that we will become some kind of emotional roadkill. Sadly, the opposite is true. Buried feelings are what kill, and buried emotional pain passes on from generation to generation.

Author's Note...

How do you feel about the use of the word "pain" in this context? Before I realized how much my childhood had impacted me emotionally, I thought anyone that talked about their emotional pain had an attitude problem. I could only understand pain as physical. I was very blocked.

A question to contemplate . . .

What childhood feelings or pain did your parents run from?

Chapter 3:

Identities Out Of Childhood Experience

Shame doesn't say we did something wrong . . . shame says we are something wrong.

-John Bradshaw

Throughout my life, I have been told I was a born teacher. Teaching comes easy to me. I have the ability to explain complicated concepts in a way that others can readily understand. I learned this skill young and out of necessity. In 1952, seven years old and a third grader, I had the most formal education in my family. If mom was in-between husbands, I was elevated to partner and confidant.

During those times, it was my job to explain things to her. For example, she needed me to clarify what the teachers wanted and why. I would translate what people meant by their humor and wisecracks. She used me as a sounding board for her worries and financial insecurity. She shared and layered me with her loneliness and anger. I collected the bittersweet responsibility tangled in her words, "I don't know what I would do without my Irene." I used the collection to build an identity.

I was learning a role that I played in all of my relationships for most of my life.

When mom had a husband (my current stepfather, John, excluded), everything changed. The man was elevated to the head of the household. I was demoted. I was expected to get back in line, squeeze myself into her "perfect family picture" and be a dutiful daughter and stepdaughter. She'd be particularly happy if I called the new man "Daddy." She struggled to keep us all fed and continually worked to explain why we girls should understand the foul moods of our stepfathers.

John, my mother's sixth husband, has been an earth angel for me. My mom and John were married when I was already out of the house and had children of my own. John was the only man mom married who didn't have a temper. In this marriage, mom became the abuser. She became paranoid and attacked with harsh criticisms. Mom physically punished John's children inappropriately. Like her with her father, John's children could not wait to move away as soon as they were old enough. John and mom are still married today, 39 years later.

Public schools and the Roman Catholic Church were our bedrocks. Everywhere we moved, Mom would immediately register us in the nearest school and find the closest church. Frequently, we heard the story of how she fought to get back to America from Portugal so that her children could be born where education and the church were free for all, including girls. Mom made sure that we had what she longed for as a child—a public school education and the Catholic Church— the church of her mother, Irene Diaz. Mom may have had only a small amount of education, but to her credit, she figured out how to get us what she had always wanted. This was the same church that her father hated and forbade my mother to attend. Mom often questioned if a priest might have abused her father when he was a boy. She felt that his rage against the church was mysteriously loaded.

I never met my grandfather. He didn't want anything to do with my mother or her children because she went against his will and moved back to America. He never changed his mind.

Mom was secure that she had given us a better childhood than she had because she didn't die and leave us motherless, and because she made sure we attended school. She believed she had given us what we needed, and in many ways she did. We were well-versed in the public education of the 50s and 60s—a time when kids and teachers were safe in the buildings, when the only illegal drugs were Luden's cough drops, and suspension meant you had been caught chewing gum. It was safe and all quite insulated from today's harsh realities.

My childhood Catholicism taught me to honor the Holy Family. I learned to love Jesus and his father, Joseph, and especially his virgin mother, Mary. The church saw to it that I learned what God did and did not expect from me.

I learned early that we were a second class Catholic family. When other parishioners rose and walked up to the altar with their heads bowed and hands clasped in prayer, my mom dutifully stayed in her pew, keeping her head bowed, knowing she was not welcome to receive the sacrament of Holy Communion—after all, she was a divorcée, and the divorced were not allowed to receive Communion. Thank goodness no one knew how many times. Nevertheless, we were tainted. Mom had committed an unpardonable mortal sin, and we were the sinner's kids.

With the emphasis on education and attendance at Mass, my sisters and I grew up to be women with advanced degrees, both in academics and shame. To paraphrase John Bradshaw from *Healing the Shame That Binds You*, shame doesn't say we did something wrong. Shame says we are something wrong.

A question for reflection . . .

What shame did you carry out of your childhood?

How does it express itself in your life today?

Chapter 4:

Stepfather and Feelings

Anger is always on top of fear, sadness, hurt or all three.

Dotty and I were 6 and 7 when Jack showed up in our lives. He brought Easter baskets for us. Tony, Mom's third husband to whom she was married at the time, was in the Merchant Marines and out to sea on a six month tour of duty. I was nervous that Tony might find out Mom had a man visiting our house on Easter Sunday morning. I had good reason to be anxious. Before Jack was ever in the picture, I was awakened in the middle of the night by Mom's screams of, "Stop hitting me, you bastard." I remember scrambling down the hallway of our tiny track ranch house just in time to watch Tony, in a fit of rage, push my mother through our living room window. I didn't know what Mom had done to make Tony push her through the window, but I knew Mom would be in even bigger trouble if Tony found out Jack was at our house. Mom kept making choices that made it difficult for me to keep her safe.

Jack was Mom's fourth husband. He was the father of my baby sister Jacqueline, who Mom had given birth to before they were married. They had to wait for her divorce from Tony to be finalized. Once we left the little ranch house to move in with Jack, I never saw Tony again. I have no idea what ever happened to him.

Jack was about 28 when he met Mom. I think she was maybe 34. Jack was handsome and Portuguese and terminally ill with an enlarged heart. He had never been married before mom and had planned on staying single due to his health.

Jack was the oldest child of an alcoholic mother and an absent father. Jack had come to America hoping to reconnect with his own father who had immigrated here. Jack's dad was like many immigrants who come to the U.S. looking for a way to support their families back in their native countries. He found more than a job. He found a new life. Jack's dad found a new job, a new house, and a new woman. Seduced by good wages and free from family obligations, he never returned to his homeland. So Jack and I had this one fact in common—we had both been abandoned by our dads.

Jack owned a red and white Studebaker Hawk sports car with a continental wheel on the back. He loved that car. He bought the car before he met my mother. It was a low riding thing that had virtually no room in the back seat. My sister Dotty and I were packed into what little space there was, which we shared with an armrest. No matter how many hours we were in that car, we were not allowed to complain. Any complaint was met with the back of Jack's hand. He could flip his arm over the back of his driver's seat and get a direct snap with his fist to the middle of a stepdaughter's cheek. Rarely, if ever, did he miss.

He was able to leave a temporary imprint on a little girl's face and a permanent mark on her self-esteem. His eyes would never leave the road, or put the car in any kind of danger. He was very agile. My mom, in the front seat holding my little sister Jackie, would remain silent. The back seat of that car was an incubator for my anger, as was our dinner table.

Jack sat at the head of the table. He made the rules and Mom made the dinner. Mom was a creative cook. She did a lot with very little. Friday nights were the most predictable, because in those days, for Catholic families, Friday meant fish for dinner. At our house, a fish dinner meant codfish, salted fillets that came in a wooden box with a lid that slid open. Mom would rinse and rinse and rinse the dried, hard pieces. Then, with mashed potatoes and Crisco cooking oil, she turned them into golden brown patties that were wonderful with ketchup. Mom used a pressure cooker, garlic, and olive oil. She steamed vegetables and knew how to cook them so they still had a crunch. My mom knew how to make food be alive with vitamins, color, and flavor. This was a real talent for a mom of the fifties.

As an adult, I can only imagine how painful it must have been for her on those days when she only had potatoes or rice to feed us. Meals rarely ended with dessert. They usually finished with Jack cracking Dotty or me across the face with his hand because we had somehow figured a way to aggravate him. I was much more skilled at pushing his limits than Dotty. I can hear Dotty pleading with me to shut up so he would stop hitting me. I never learned to keep quiet, and he never learned to stop hitting me. I silently imagined him dead.

Anger is a feeling, an emotion. It doesn't come alone. It comes attached to fear, sadness, hurt, or all three. When we are young or vulnerable, and we have no power, anger offers an illusion of power. Unable to face our underlying feelings, we detach from the fear, sadness, and hurt. Instead, we remold our anger like pieces of clay. We reshape and reshape until we have dried hard bricks of resentments. These resentment bricks are what we use to build the walls around our hearts; walls of rage.

Throughout our childhood, we build these walls of rage one experience at a time. My rage seduced me into believing my anger wasn't anger, but rather, my drive to succeed. I mistook it for motivation. Maybe at some level it was, but it exacted a high price. The price it often exacted was my inability to listen, or to see opportunity, because I was blinded by my anger. It left me very stubborn.

Determined to someday get free from the back seat of that damn Studebaker, to get out of my family and to never eat another meal at that table, I fantasized how differently I would treat my children. I imagined a family of my own, doing and having everything I wasn't getting. My kids were going to get the life I wished I had. My children would have a great dad who played with them. I would never get divorced or let my children have a stepfather and feel like extra baggage in their own family.

Jack was determined not to abandon Jacqueline, his daughter, the way he had been deserted by his father. With the clock ticking away the healthy minutes of his heart, he parented my little sister with love and attention. At the end, when he was confined to his bed for most of his waking hours, Jacqueline would crawl up beside him and they would play paper dolls and have tea parties for hours. He would read her books and they would make up stories for her dolls. Jacqueline was his only way into the future. He knew that his heart had very little time left.

Jack and I had one other thing in common; we both loved my little sister, Jacqueline. Dotty and I watched this father and daughter relationship unfold. Jack gave Jacqueline every bit of heart he was able to give. He died when Jacqueline was five years old.

So many times I had wished he would leave. Now he was gone forever and Jackie didn't have her daddy. I felt guilty and scared.

A question for reflection . . .

What feelings are under your anger?

Chapter 5:

Prelude to Marriage

Doing what we always do, getting what we always get—one generation to the next, traditions and insanity are hard to separate.

My first husband, Kevin Wilson, is Lynn and Shawn Mary's biological father. He was twenty-six when we met and I was seventeen. He was charming, handsome, and fun-loving. Under the influence of alcohol, he became a very different man. Kevin's mother died giving birth to him and his father, often described as the "town drunk," died shortly afterwards. There were no relatives to take Kevin in for the first four years of his life. He became a ward of the state and eventually a product of the Massachusetts foster care system.

Kevin had very few memories from his early years. He had blocked most of them out. He did have one vivid scene that he hadn't lost. He saw himself not tall enough to reach the top of a kitchen table. He was stretching as hard as he could from his tiptoes trying to get some of the food that was on the table. He recalled that there were many other bigger children around the table, and no one was helping him. The next memory he could access was ten years later. Everything in-between was a blank. His second memory was that of an office where he was being adopted by an older couple that he later learned were distant cousins of his mother.

Kevin's adopted parents were wealthy and cold. They used every opportunity possible to remind Kevin how fortunate he was that they had "taken him in." Initially, I was impressed by their beautiful home and the roasted duck they served at Christmas. However, I quickly grew to dislike what I judged to be their mean-spiritedness towards Kevin. I felt protective of him whenever we were at their house. Often on our drive home, I would try to get him to see how cruel their comments were. He would staunchly defend them while reiterating their sentiments of how lucky he was that they "took him in." This was just one of the many ways we disagreed.

People raised in crazy family environments have little difficulty finding each other to mate. Kevin and I were no exception. It never ceases to amaze me how classic my behavior has been. Why? Why do we do it? Why do we marry the same men our mothers married? Why do we fall in love with the same women our fathers struggled with? Why do we find alcoholics or drug addicts when we lived the devastation with these diseases as children? We all swore we wouldn't, and yet so many of us did. We repeated what we knew. The packages that our new relationships came wrapped in often looked so different from what we were raised with yet when we opened them, after the pink cloud of the new romance had passed, we were looking right into the eye of our history. We were repeating history. I guess we repeat it until we wake up to it. Until we own our history and the imprint it had on us, we are destined to relive it.

Two forces were at play when I decided to marry Kevin—hormones and the Catholic Church. At seventeen years old, I was a virgin. It was the summer between my high school graduation and my freshman year in college. Full of anticipation, I looked forward to the fall when I would be off to college and no longer responsible for anyone but myself.

During that summer of 1963, I worked as a waitress in a local 24-hour diner. The hours were long, and the tips were good enough to ensure that I'd have sufficient money for college tuition. What I hadn't planned on were the complications a summer romance would provide.

Kevin was a town cop. He looked great in his navy blue uniform. We began dating and I was proud as a peacock. An older guy was asking me out. Could I be any cooler? I thought not.

As a child, the Catholic Church offered me a safe haven. I loved the ritual of the Mass. It was predictable—the bells were rung, the Communion served. One of my favorite parts happened at the end of the Mass. I loved when the priest blanketed the "Go in peace" over everyone as we prepared to exit the sanctuary back into the world. I trusted it. It gave me the stability that was missing at home. I followed the rules. I found them to be comforting. The priests assured us that they spoke the words of God. That worked for me. I needed someone bigger than me to be in charge. Without safe adults at home, I needed someone who knew what they were doing, and who better than God? That, along with the ritual, structure, and order, made me feel safe. In my mind, the church and God were one and the same. They were not separate. I devoutly loved both.

I wanted to be a "good girl." I was convinced that if I were a good enough girl, life at home would get easier. Being a "good girl" would bring honor to our family. Mom would be happier and not make so many poor decisions. And maybe her daughters would be enough, and she wouldn't have to find another husband.

My summer was filled with conflicting needs. My need to be a "good girl" was constantly wrestling with my adolescent needs. Drive-in theatres . . . warm summer nights . . . a '55 Chevy . . . kissy-face . . . and emerging passions were all complicating my life. How do I live in my body and keep the church happy? How do I be a "good girl" and a passionate female at the same time? I wrestled with the urges produced by my sexually healthy young body. At seventeen, the only force stronger than my sexuality was the fear I held of getting pregnant and thereby dishonoring my family, upsetting Father Riley our parish priest, and worst of all, causing my mother more pain.

September came, and I was still a virgin—not an easy task. Off to school I went. Cape Cod Community College—here I come. Kevin and my mother followed me. They didn't follow me physically, just emotionally. They stalked me, phone call after phone call of, "Come on home, why do you need college?" Mom called daily. "I miss you. I need you at home. Go to school around here." Kevin also wanted me home, and meanwhile, my sexual curiosity was peaking. So I began to ask myself, "Why am I here at school?" And then I'd quickly remind myself, "Oh yeah, I was elected to student government. I received an A on my first English paper." I was torn. I liked school, but it was a new experience for me to be away from home and not taking care of my family. Kevin wanted me to come home. My mom wanted me to come home. The church says no sex outside of marriage. Sex is for procreation only. Good girls know that. I made an appointment with the Dean of Women. On November 1, 1963, I was officially on my way back home after having been at college less than seventy-five days!

Three weeks later, President John F. Kennedy was shot. Four months after that, Kevin and I were married. In the tradition of a "good Catholic girl," I was careful not to use birth control. Nine months after the sacrament of marriage, the first of my "Irish twins" was born. The second was born thirteen months later. I was honoring the Catholic manual to a "T"—honor and obey your parents, the church, and now, my husband.

A question for reflection . . .

What family "traditions/insanity" have you continued?

Chapter 6:

The Broken Dream

Just put on a happy face.

March 1964 - 9:30 a.m.

"Irene, I'm going up to the square to get some cigarettes. Be right back. What time is dinner tonight?"

"Kevin, I told everyone to come around six o'clock. I'm excited. I'm making sauce from scratch using fresh tomatoes."

"Yeah, well, I might stop by the station and see what's happening. See if I'm on the detail schedule."

"Will you bring some grated Parmesan cheese home? I think I have everything else. I'm really excited—scared too. This is going to be so great. Are you excited?"

"Yeah, yeah . . . look, I gotta get going."

"Ok, ok, I'm sorry. I'm just really looking forward to tonight. I wish I didn't feel so queasy. I don't even want a cigarette with my tea. Just want the tea."

Kevin grabbed his jacket and keys, quickly finished his last bit of coffee, closed the door behind him, and moved quietly down the stairs to his beloved Chevy waiting for him on the gravel driveway.

I spent the day cleaning every square inch of our tiny two-bedroom apartment. We lived above a carriage house on a beautiful estate in rural Massachusetts, just a few miles outside the main center of town with no public transportation. Kevin had the only car between us. I was accustomed to not having a car. Mom only let me drive her car when she had an errand for me to run. The sauce was bubbling in the pot on the stove. It filled the kitchen with a wonderful smell that fed my anticipation for the meal that was to come. I wished I felt better, but I just kept feeling like I was going to throw up. I knew I wouldn't, but I still felt like I was carsick.

When the food was ready, I unwrapped a box of table linens from our wedding gift pile. They were stiff and bright white. The old hand-me-down kitchen set was freshly polished. The scratches had been nicely muted by the gloss of new wax. The table was pretty. I knew it looked pretty. Mom's rules were "Always make the table look pretty, even if it is just us." But tonight it wasn't just "us." It would be three other couples. All of Kevin's best buddies and their wives were coming. These six people had been at our wedding just the month prior. The guys were the groomsmen.

I never saw this kind of preparation at my house as a child. Mom never had couples over. I was so pumped. But where was Kevin? It was 2:30 p.m. and he wasn't back yet. No call. I excused his lateness with the idea that he must have met up with some of the guys from the station. They loved to have coffee and hang out. Those part-time cops were quite a team. He loved those guys.

I wonder how much spaghetti to cook? How much does this stuff blow up to? I'm sure I don't cook it till much later. How do you get everything on the table hot? I bet those other wives know how to do this. God, it's late . . . 4:45 p.m. What the hell is he doing? Why doesn't he call? I need the damn cheese. I'll get dressed. He has to be here soon.

6:00 p.m.

"Hi guys, come on in. I'm not sure where Kevin is. He left hours ago to get cigarettes and . . . oh, there he is. He's pulling in the driveway now."

Everyone turned as Kevin's brakes stopped the car abruptly. The gravel made wakes behind the tires. "Hey guy, where ya' been? Irene says you've been gone for hours," Peter, his best friend teased. "Running out on your new bride already?" Kevin smiled. He dropped his Camel cigarette to the ground, mashed it with the bottom of his maroon-red penny loafer, and asked me to come into the bedroom with him for a minute. He invited the others to get themselves a beer.

The bedroom was tiny. I started to ask, "Where have you been?" He grabbed my arm and pushed me against the wall. His face was right in mine. The smell of a man who had been drinking beer and smoking cigarettes for the last nine hours filled the room. The merciless smell sunk immediately to the bottom of my belly.

"I don't want to hear any complaining from you, bitch. Don't you ever make me look bad in front of my friends again. Now, you get out there and make dinner." The nausea from that smell was validation that I was pregnant.

I immediately did what I watched my mom do for years. I put on a smile, sucked in my breath, and followed Kevin back into our living room. I was completely disconnected from my feelings and acted like everything was fine. It had to be. I had told myself I was never going to live my mother's life. I was never going to give my children the family life she gave me. I began creating my own picture of the perfect family life. It was no longer my mother shoving me into her picture—now I was cramming myself into my own fantasy.

When the student is ready, the teacher appears.

About two and a half years later . . .

The front page of the town newspaper pictured a local woman being arrested for the murder of her husband. The story alleged that she had picked up a knife from her dish rack and before he could get one more punch to her face, while he had her back pressed hard against her kitchen counter, she stuck the knife in his belly. He was dead when the police arrived.

A second photograph showed her two young children being shuffled into a vehicle that was clearly designated official with the seal of the Commonwealth of Massachusetts.

I knew what motivated that woman. I knew how she summoned up enough hate to stick a knife in her drunken husband. When a man, insane with alcohol and stronger than you, is punching your face and head, every instinct in your body wants to find a way to hurt him back. The warrior in the bottom of my belly completely identified with the front page mother.

Those two newspaper pictures scared me. I could be in the paper next. I didn't want my children in a sheriff's car. I never wanted to see my children taken away from me. I knew that if I fought back, that is exactly what would happen.

Kevin was a local cop. They protected their own. They didn't even give him citations for drunk driving. The few times I called them to the house, they told me to leave until he sobered up. They chastised me for making such a big deal of our "domestic problems."

I knew exactly how the "newspaper woman" felt. I silently thanked her in my heart and prayed for her safety. I felt warned by her presence on the front page of the paper that sat on my kitchen counter.

Barely three weeks later, Kevin was sleeping off a drunken stupor. The house was quiet—quiet with the deafening silence that follows a night of domestic violence. My face throbbed. My right eye was swollen almost shut. My balance was thrown off by my impaired vision. What was I going to do? I didn't want this life for my girls. I needed help. I wanted someone to tell me how to make Kevin stop drinking and how to stop the craziness at our house. I had to make my marriage work. I was willing to do whatever it took.

I called the only place I knew to call, the place I had gone to for answers and rules my whole life.

"Hi, my name is Irene, and I take Communion at your church. I was wondering if I could have an appointment today with one of the priests."

"Could you please tell me what this is in regards to?"

"It's about my marriage. My husband and I are having some problems. I really need to talk to a priest today."

"Okay, well, what about one o'clock. He'll see you at the rectory right after his lunch. Can you make it then?"

I said I'd be there, thanked her, and hung up.

I put the girls in the stroller and walked the two miles to the local rectory. I needed to talk to the priest.

My face hurts. God, I hate walking up to the church looking like this. I'll wear sunglasses and a hat. Irene, get over it. Very few people in this town know you. You haven't been here a year yet. They won't notice. Oh my eye is so sore. I'll put more ice on it later.

"Mommy boo-boo? Daddy hit? No, no hit."

"Daddy is sorry honey. Daddy no hit anymore."

What am I going to do? How do I get out of this mess? What can I do for money? Why can't I have one of those mothers or fathers who gives their kids money? Why couldn't I be born to parents that help their kids financially? When I get out of this mess, I'll always help my kids out with money.

I hate Kevin right now. Oh God, I never wanted my girls to see this. I never wanted them to have this craziness in their home. Nice job, Irene. You've given the girls what you grew up in. They don't deserve to live like this—drunken rages waking everyone up in the night, hearing their mom being pushed around—the hitting and kicking.

(I mistakenly believed that because the girls were so young they wouldn't remember the violence and it wouldn't affect them. Sadly, years later, I learned how much trauma children do somatize in their bodies and it does greatly affect them.)

The priest will help. He will guide me. He will give me direction. I just need to hang on till I see him.

"Hello, Father, I'm Irene. These are my two girls. Lynn is two years old and Shawn Mary is one."

"Well, hello girls. You certainly have your hands full. Now, have you been in my office before? Do we know each other?"

"Not really Father, but I have been receiving Holy Communion here for about a year. I came from St Anne's church with Father Riley."

"Oh, yes, Father Riley. He's in a retirement home now. Did you know that?"

"Yes Father, my mother told me."

"So, what is it I can do for you? What happened to your face?"

"Well, Father, that's why I'm here. My husband's done this to me a couple of times. He comes home drunk and goes into a rage. I've come to ask your guidance."

"Well, my dear, what have you done to make him so angry?"

WHAT?! My mind snapped. I went black with rage and my voice froze.

He did not just say that. He couldn't have just said that. I am here because, all of my life, I have done everything his church has told me to do. And this is what he says to me? What have I done to make my husband so angry? Not as much as I would like to do to you, you bastard!

I have no idea what else he said. I think he mumbled something about praying to the Blessed Mother. Maybe I just made that up. I wanted out. I wanted out of his office. I wanted out of that building. I wanted out of that church. I wanted out of my marriage. And I wanted out of any further relationship with God.

That day I drew a line in the sand. Kevin, the Catholic Church, and God were on one side of the line. The girls and I were on the other.

Questions to contemplate . . .

What family picture have you tried to paint?

What have you done with crisis—with change?

Chapter 7:

Leaving the Broken Dream

Rage often dresses a lot like determination.

I didn't know it at the time, but it was from this place, my side of the line, this place in the void, that I began my trek towards the light. When I was in it, I could only see the blackness of the void. I saw no options—no way out. I had no answers—just questions.

How will I feed my girls? Where can we live? Who will watch them while I work? What will I do for work? How did I get here? I had good S.A.T. scores. I was considered one of the "bright" kids. Kids from advanced placement classes are not supposed to become single teenage moms. They are supposed to know better. How could I have screwed up so badly? How could I have given my girls such a loser for a mother?

So where do you go when your world crumbles, when everything you believed and trusted betrays you, when the sun rises in the evening and the snow falls in the summer, and when the world makes no sense whatsoever? Where do you go? Me—I went home to my mother's house.

Less than three years after my triumphant march out of her house and down the Catholic Church aisle, now with my tail between my legs, I

43

was back at Mom's kitchen table, only this time, I had two babies with me—and they were mine. They were mine morning, noon, and night. They were mine holidays and cloudy days and sunny days. They were mine when I was alert and they were mine when I was tired. They were mine. Kevin had never really been involved with the girls when we were together. A truth I had denied. This truth was now in my face. The girls were mine.

I hated. I hated. I hated. I hated Kevin. I hated the Catholic Church. I hated my mother for not stopping me from getting married at a young age. I hated everything around me.

I hated Kevin for never giving me any money, for not trying to stop drinking, for not showing up for the girls, for being just like my father. The one constant Kevin knew from his mother and father was abandonment. Granted they left because of death and alcoholism, but the reasons make little difference to a small boy forming his idea of the world. All he knew was that they left. This time I was the one leaving him. His wife was walking out the door and taking his daughters with her.

Kevin worked a night shift. Under the advice of an attorney, I moved out while Kevin was at work. With the help of my stepfather, John, I packed up everything I could fit into a small truck and was gone when Kevin returned from work. I left him one of everything; one chair, one knife, one fork, one plate, one bed, one set of sheets. I was not legally entitled to anything we owned. That was why the attorney advised me to leave in the night. This was before laws were changed and women gained more legal rights in divorce settlements. Kevin didn't fight for anything that I took from the house, including his daughters. No one ever fought for him. He kept our house and car. Over the phone, he asked me to come back and I refused. This time I was done. After the divorce was finalized, we had very little contact. He sold the house and moved a hundred miles away from where the girls and I lived. In the beginning, whenever I was in his presence, which was three or four times over two years, I was traumatized with fear and rage. My body would shake uncontrollably. He visited the girls three or four times at most and then he faded into the void. Years later, I was blessed with good therapists who helped me heal physically. I was able to release that old trauma from my body.

My father never came after my mother to find my sister and me. He never pursued us. He never showed up. So what did I give my girls? I gave them what I knew—a father who never showed up, a father who abandoned them. Kevin and I both gave our daughters what we knew. Generation on to generation, we pass down what we know until we learn something different and have the courage to then live that difference.

Money was tight. Daycare cost $75 a week. If I had a good week, I made $100 waiting on tables. At this rate, I wondered how I would ever get out of my mother's house? I couldn't afford a decent car, and I couldn't keep mine on the road. How would I get to work? Kevin never sent the money he had been court ordered to send.

At this point, my mother was in a new marriage (with John) and had gained four stepchildren with this marriage. Her house was in total chaos.

For starters, the house wasn't big enough for the "new" family before the girls and I arrived. The rooms were small and there weren't enough of them. There was one full bathroom for ten people, three of whom were teenage girls. And these teenage girls had no plans on doing anything Mom had in mind for them, while she had no understanding of what it was to be a teenage girl with a new stepmom. Mom was fighting with everyone pretty much nonstop, and, as if all of that wasn't miserable enough for our reconfigured family, the well that supplied the house with water went dry the week I arrived with my girls! We were overstaying our welcome the day we arrived. I had to find another place to live. But where?

A friend from college, Diane, came by to catch up on my life. I was embarrassed. I felt like such a failure. She was in my wedding party. The dresses were pretty. The boneless breast of chicken wasn't bad. The band was fun. How did the marriage go so wrong?

I hated. I hated. I chewed on my hate. I called it resolve. I would somehow—some way—get out of the mess that had become my life. I would survive.

How much was I fighting for my girls and how much was I fighting to protect my pride? The last place I wanted to go was to the welfare office. I remembered the visits from the social worker when I was a kid. The "worker" ordered my sister and I to get our state- issued rubber boots out of our closet. She wanted verification that my mom had not squandered the voucher money on something wild and frivolous, like milk or bread.

Here I was ten years later. I hated really hard that day. I hated being in that office. I hated that they had so little to offer. I hated that I was sitting where my mother had sat. I hated my way out. I never took the aid. My pride wouldn't let me.

After some stalled starts, I was blessed with a job in a predominantly black United Way-sponsored daycare center, located in the middle of Roxbury, Massachusetts. My girls qualified to attend the same center on a sliding fee scale basis. I was able to afford the tuition. We also found an apartment with the only white family in an all black neighborhood.

Soon, I marched the three of us into an African-American Episcopal Church. I went to the church for two reasons. One, I wanted to give the girls a church community to be a part of. Two, I wanted to get myself officially excommunicated from the Catholic Church.

The Roxbury community challenged and blessed us in many ways. My favorite blessing came in the form of a grant from President Lyndon Johnson's War On Poverty program. I was given some free tuition money to attend college and begin my work towards a degree in early childhood education. Hope had arrived. For the next twenty years, a college education became one of the gods of my understanding—my higher power. A degree was what I trusted. I was going to bust out over the wall of poverty, divorce, crummy cars, and nasty apartments. I was building my ladder with textbooks and I was climbing out. Nothing was going to stop me, certainly not a human limitation like fatigue.

I worked full-time, studied part-time, played with my girls often, cleaned my apartment, did the laundry, shopped, cooked the meals, and made straight As. These were not difficult tasks because I had found a little helper. I added another god to my list of idols, a little pill called Black Beauty. You might know her by her other street name—Speed. In Roxbury Speed was easy to find and like any good addict I justified the expense. My rationale was convincing myself it made me more productive. No longer was I the naïve young virgin who married Kevin. Now I was an angry, determined woman of the sixties. The hate I chewed was forming a stiff, dried leather vest around my heart.

During this time, there was a second woman in a newspaper article who significantly impacted my life. One winter afternoon, I had just finished a typing job that I took on for extra money. I was waiting in a frigid, Boston snowstorm for a bus. I was tired and concerned about getting to the sitter on time to pick up the girls. It was getting late. While waiting, I read the evening paper. There on the front page was a story about a woman who was angry that she could not wear a pants suit to work. She was mad that she was required to wear a skirt or dress on the job while men were allowed to wear what they chose. She had taken her complaint to court.

As I stood on that Boston corner dressed in a skirt and nylons, with my legs stinging from the cold, I thought—wow—she took her complaint to court. *I, on the other hand, had never once considered questioning the rule.* Flash, the light went on big time, actually more than a light—an all points bulletin. It was as if a chain of dominoes, lined up in my brain, began to fall. They fell in a perfect, choreographed sequence, one domino after another—one rule after the next. From that moment on, I never stopped questioning the rules or the authorities that pronounce them.

More than ever, I was determined to make my own rules. No one was going to tell me what to think or how to behave. I did everything but burn my bra; I couldn't afford to.

While going to school with the support of my buddy Speed, I started double dating with another seductive chemical and companion—*alcohol*. I compared my drinking to Kevin's and convinced myself I was handling it well. A no-brainer, I conceded. It was apples and oranges. There was no comparison. I paid the bills. I showed up at work and school and for my girls. I didn't have a D.W.I. I was over 21 and free to do as I pleased. I wasn't hurting anyone, and anyway, I needed some relaxation.

That first year I was taking the "diet pills" in the morning to get going, really enjoying great "energy" and no appetite, willing to accept such dry mouth I believed my tongue was going to be permanently stuck to the roof of my mouth. Then drinking wine after work so I could shut my head off by 11 or 12 at night. I did love the false energy and the weight loss. Thank God I only lasted on speed for about a year. The physical side effects—a racing heart and dry mouth—eventually frightened me into stopping. But I only stopped the speed. I would keep alcohol in my daily life for many more years.

I was cutting my own cloth. My mom never relied on alcohol nor did any of her husbands. This was my own deal. I bolstered myself with a sense of achievement for my grocery store stemware and tasteful gallon jugs of Gallo wine. I loved having friends from work or college classes over for spaghetti dinners and Chianti. You couldn't claim a stake in the sixties if you didn't have a straw wrapped Chianti bottle, layered with melted wax as a candleholder, artfully placed in the middle of your kitchen table.

I had arrived. I was a new me. Ok, there was one divorce and one abusive husband, but the girls and I were on the right track now. I was not going to be my mother, and my girls were not going to get a repeat of my childhood. I had set a new course and I was on it with a vengeance.

A question to contemplate . . .

Have you ever reinvented yourself?

Chapter 8:

New Life

The trick question for all relationships . . .

How do you show up for others without losing yourself?

The first day I moved the girls and myself into our Roxbury apartment, I put their yard toys out in our tiny postage stamp backyard. I use the term "backyard" loosely. It was a bit of extra ground left over after the garbage cans were lined up. Anyway, after putting the toys in the yard, I went back into the house to help them finish unpacking their stuff. We spent about an hour in the apartment.

By that time, the girls had enough of "helping Mommy." They wanted to go outside. I told them they had to stay in the yard, and I showed them what I meant by yard. It took the three of us about thirty seconds to realize that every single bike, push toy, shovel, and bucket was gone. Stolen. It was surreal. Not one scrap of evidence that any toys had ever been there. I felt like I was in a movie. We were being filmed. I was the pioneer woman on the prairie and somehow, someway, the Indians were watching my every move. They knew all about me; and I knew nothing about them. That was our welcome to the city.

We tried to invite neighbor children to come over to play. I wanted the girls to have friends. There were precious few kids who were allowed to come into our house. Most of the children were not allowed in other people's homes. The neighborhood parents kept a tight reign on their kids' whereabouts. They wanted their kids in plain view, right where they could see them. That usually meant in their own apartments. I soon learned why—a young boy in the neighborhood exposed himself to the girls and they ran home screaming. I finally got it. There was no playing in the neighborhood. We were not in the suburbs anymore, and I had to wise up.

When I look back now, I am struck with how young and clueless I was. I am also horrified at the danger to which I naively exposed the girls. It is obvious to me that we have been blessed with a band of angels who have kept us protected, and I did not make their job easy.

Later it became a joke with my friends (black and white) that there was always a parking space in front of my house. They all surmised it was because the last car there had just been stolen.

As unsafe as my neighborhood was, the girls and I have many fond memories of our three years in that apartment. We could have really tall Christmas trees because the ceilings were so high. I remember having a great decorate-the-tree party and me being the only one at the party without a date. It was a fun night with good people, yummy food, and of course, plenty of wine. We still love flipping through those old yellowed Polaroids with their curled edges. We had the entire cities of Boston and Cambridge just a bus fare and subway token away. We used the parks and museums and took advantage of the public pools and free concerts. For the price of a cup of tea, two juices, and three cookies, we could fill an afternoon with adventures.

That was part of our story. But I also recall some other scenes. I can remember the people sitting across from me on trains who carried briefcases or suitcases and backpacks, all teasing me with possibility. They were symbols of opportunity. They were living lives much different than mine. On good days, I imagined myself with a briefcase and a suitcase, packed with my degree, on my way somewhere important.

On P.M.S. days, I felt trapped and broke and stuck. I was a hamster on a wheel, spinning nowhere, with homework, daycare bills, no time to call my own, and two little girls fifteen years away from independence. I harbored a sick, empty feeling of remorse. Like in the moment after you drop a dish and watch it shatter on the floor, or you bring your eyes back to the road and realize you are going to hit the car in front of you, or you watch the train you were supposed to be on pull out of the station without you, I was permeated with a cellular feeling of oops. I had misplaced my trust. I had completely, no-holds-barred, put my trust down on the wrong number. I felt like one of those old ladies down in Florida who gives her life savings over the phone to a con man. The carnival had come through town, and I had believed it. Why didn't I know better?

None of my friends from college were married, much less divorced with two children. They didn't marry the first guy that turned them on. Some of them had been raised Catholic, and yet they didn't follow every rule. No, they used the pill or diaphragms. They didn't think having children without getting an education first was a good idea. Not a good idea for the children. Not a good idea for the mother.

How could I have been so dumb? How could I have put myself in this predicament? And worse, how could I have done this to my children?

Whenever I started going down this road of thinking, a couple of glasses of wine always seemed like a good idea. I rationalized that I deserved it. I worked hard. I deserved a little pleasure. What I didn't own was that the wine kept me from feeling what I didn't want to feel.

A question to contemplate . . .

How do you hide from yourself?

Chapter 9:

The Children and Me

We don't see things as they are . . . We see things as we are.
-Anais Nin

The social worker at the girls' Roxbury preschool/daycare center was my first (though not my last) call from a school authority. I worked as a teaching assistant for the same organization at another site.

"Hi Ms. Wilson, this is Lindsey Peterson from the daycare center. I'm the social worker and . . . no, no, nothing is wrong . . . Lynn and Shawn are fine. Nothing serious, but I need you to stop in my office to talk with me about Lynn. It should only take a few minutes. Will you have enough time this afternoon when you come to pick up the girls? I don't want you to miss your connecting bus."

I assured her I could make a later connection, and she reassured me the girls were fine.

What does she want? What can it be? Irene, what do you think? You are divorced. You and your kids are a statistic. Lynnie loved her dad and she never sees him. You gave your kids a deadbeat dad. It must be hard for her, being one of the few white kids in the whole daycare, but she and Shawn love going. They love their friends. What is it? There's my bus.

When I arrived at Ms. Peterson's office, we exchanged the normal pleasantries; she quickly got to the point of my visit.

"Well . . . I need to let you know that we have some concerns about Lynn. She has been acting out aggressively with some of the other kids. Particularly the boys."

"What do you mean aggressively?"

"Well . . . she hits and can be fairly disruptive. And sometimes she won't listen to her teacher. Her behavior isn't that bad. But we just think something is up. This is a change for her. How is everything at home? Has anything changed?"

"No, not really. She hasn't seen her dad in a long time. I know she misses him. He never comes to see them. I didn't have my dad. I'm just sick that she and Shawn get stuck living in a divorced family like me. I hated that my mom was married and divorced a lot. I never wanted this for my kids. But their father was violent. We had to leave. They're safe now. Things are calm now at our home. We live together, just the three of us. We have relatives that live in the apartment above us. They help watch the girls. She seems okay at home."

"Maybe you can talk to her when you get home. See if she has anything she wants to share. We'll keep an eye on her here and keep you posted."

Ugh, my heart sank—the word was out, Lynn was only four years old and the authorities were telling me that she had problems. She was not perfect. That would be Lynn, my daughter, my first-born. I would be the mother, the mother who is in college studying early childhood development. The one who is supposed to be learning the answers?

Well, she was perfect when I got her. She was perfect as a baby. So what happened? Who screwed up? Oh this was it, my first big official dose of "parent guilt." I had screwed up. It is declared. They have it in her permanent file, and she hasn't even reached first grade.

I didn't know it at the time, but this conversation established an echo. A nagging, critical voice moved into my head that day. It continued to relentlessly monitor my parenting for 25 more years. What I heard Ms. Peterson say was, "Your daughter is in deep emotional pain. You and your poor choice of a father for her caused it. She will never be happy. She will never have any friends. She will most likely become a bag lady, and it is your fault. You promised yourself at eight years old that you would never get divorced and look what you did, how will this child ever make it?"

I talked to Lynn when we got home. I asked her how her day went. She said fine. She said that one of the boys was bothering her. I didn't stay there long with her. I got right into telling her that I understood she missed her daddy and I knew she didn't want us to be divorced. And then I explained to this four-year-old child how there was no other option. Her daddy and I had to get divorced because we weren't safe with him. I let her know that I felt the same way she did when I was a little girl. And I told her more than once that her feelings were okay.

What I didn't do was listen. I would not learn how to listen for many years. I still have to work at listening. At the time, all I could see and hear was my own history. I couldn't separate my daughter's story from my own. I never wanted my parents to be divorced. I wanted my father at the dinner table every night. I wanted my dad to pick me up when he came home. I wanted to know what it was like to be swooped up on top of my daddy's shoulders. I wanted to feel the combination of height and love. I wanted to know what it felt like to belong to a loving, biological father.

The little girl of my childhood, who I had long before locked away in the back room of my heart, was silently screaming her longings. She was projecting them all over my daughter. The part of me that was supposed to be the grown-up couldn't hear anything but the demands of my own unmet childhood needs. I not only wanted a "real" dad who was emotionally available in my life, but I also wanted a mom who was aware enough to validate my feelings.

So I validated Lynn. I assured her that I knew what she was feeling and why she acted out at school. In other words, I told her how she felt. I then washed the whole situation down with a big dose of guilt.

Guilt and worry were always a part of the ritual. It was a tonic that I immediately swallowed when my kids were in trouble.

I did anything but recognize that she and I were two different people. And her experience of the world was not mine. Therefore, her feelings were not the same as mine, and her needs were not necessarily what I needed at her age.

It would be fourteen years before I found out what caused Lynn's aggressive acting out in the daycare center that day.

The social worker was right. Lynn was different. Something had changed. She was testing, taunting, teasing, and pushing the limits. As I sit here in my office thirty-five years later looking back, it is as if I am looking down a long hallway. I am straining to see and hear what was going on. There are images, but they are vague and fleeting. Why aren't they clearer? I know it was a long time ago, but I can easily recall older images, which are of much less importance to me.

No, it isn't the eraser of time that has dulled these images. I wish that were my excuse. I know why I can't remember. I can't remember because I wasn't there. Yes, I was there physically, but I wasn't there emotionally. My girls didn't have me emotionally and I didn't have me emotionally. I was continually distracted.

Understandably, I was wrapped up in a world of survival that was fed by need, but it was also fed by ambition and anger and pride. I can't specify how Lynn changed, because at the time I was consumed with my agenda of being an independent, single mom who was well-educated and financially self-sufficient. And to divert me even more, this independent woman was gradually becoming dependent on wine and cigarettes.

My conscious game plan was to keep my eye on the ball, keep my eye on the prizes. The first prize was to get a degree, and the second prize was to never be dependent on a man again. My goal was to not be like my mother. I prided myself in not chasing my mother's fantasy of a perfect-happily-ever-after-husband-and-white-picket-fence-family-with-the-stay-at-home-mother.

I had myself convinced that all of my hard work was to benefit the girls. To be fair to myself, I was working to provide for them. But, the part of my drive I did not own was the part that was fueled by my unmet childhood needs. Without my awareness or permission, I was fulfilling an underlying script that had been buried since childhood

Buried is another word for denial. I had much that was buried. My shovel was well worn. No matter how long ago or how deep I had buried those painful feelings, memories, and unmet needs, they continually wriggled to the surface. These buried feelings became my unspoken agenda. I never felt completely safe or finished. I carried a low level feeling of anxiety squirming in the bottom of my belly, pushing me to continually seek the next goal or accomplishment. I was not able to articulate my needs, not to anyone else, much less myself. I was continually searching for some kind of peace while living at a level of high alert. This was the norm I brought out of my childhood.

Eventually, I projected my feelings of incompleteness onto the girls. I pushed them around by my needs for everyone to be happy. To me, happy meant safe. I wanted everyone out of harm's way. Sounds appropriate, except my definition of "harm's way" kept changing. Growing up in an unstable environment left me with a low tolerance level for struggle on one hand, while on the other I carried an expectation that struggle would be the norm. I had an internal radar system that was unnecessarily on high alert.

My dilemma was this: I had an expressed goal of getting an education and not being dependent on a man. This agenda was clear to me and everyone else. But along with this expressed agenda was an underlying urgency that I can only describe as a compelling need to be doing something more, better, and different than whatever I was doing. I lived yearning to quiet this old uneasy echo.

Questions to contemplate . . .

If you let your fear talk to you, what does it say?

How much of what it says is an old story?

**SECTION TWO:
UNDERSTANDING
OURSELVES**

Chapter 10:

Crazy Families and Feelings

Why do we want to run from feelings, if feelings are the language of our experience?
Why do we want to avoid this information?

Our egos are built to want to feel good. And we are raised in a culture that doesn't only want to feel good, but wants the good feelings immediately. Feelings come in a mixed bag. Some feel better than others. However, all feelings come with information for us. To ignore or avoid our feelings is like not opening our mail. There are consequences.

We are also a culture that worships the mind. We are afraid to trust our intuition. We believe intellect and reason are the Higher Power. We treat them like gods. Feelings are not logical. So as a culture, at best, we treat feelings with suspicion; at worst, we ignore and fight our feelings as if they were the enemy.

Ok, let's recap:

1) We have been programmed to chase only good feelings and want them immediately.

2) We have been programmed to trust only our intellect.

3)   We shut off our uncomfortable feelings.

Human beings are made up of mind, body, and spirit. To live exclusively from our intellect is like being an eight-cylinder engine but firing on only three. We are missing the power that is possible and making the ride a lot harder than it needs to be.

If you were raised in a crazy family where no one taught you to identify or cope with your feelings, then your childhood fear gave you an added reason for trying to avoid feelings—one that I think is particularly pertinent. Let me explain.

Feelings are vibration. They cause movement. For example, love makes us shaky in the knees; joy can make us laugh so hard we fear wetting our pants. Betrayal can so intensely stun us we are sure we feel the walls of our chest caving in. Pride for our children's success pushes our hearts to a wider capacity than we ever thought possible. Feelings are movement.

When you are growing up in a crazy family, no one is teaching you to identify your feelings. Feelings are not being discussed, nor are they being validated. However, you are seeing some feelings modeled… usually the extremes of feelings, such as rage or hysterical outbursts— followed by silence. No one talks about what just happened or what happened the night before. The tension can hang so heavy in the air we have to duck to clear it, yet no one mentions it.

Because of these extreme swings and lack of guidance, we developed very little tolerance for the vibration of feelings. We didn't want any "boat to rock," keeping everything still and calm became our consistent goal. We learned to fear any change in the emotional environment. Movement usually signaled trouble, we feared an imposing escalation would soon fill the room. Feelings meant movement, movement meant escalation, and escalation meant someone could get hurt!

I use the following diagram to illustrate this phenomenon.

Emotional outbursts are represented with jagged vertical lines. Flat lines represent the predictable silence that often follows.

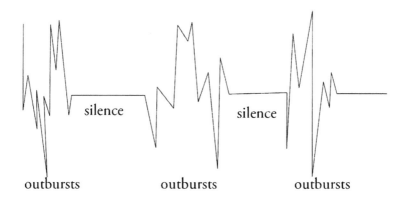

Remember children learn how to identify feelings from their parents. Albeit a simplification, these are basically the emotional options modeled for a kid growing up in crazy family. They get to choose either the insanity of the outbursts

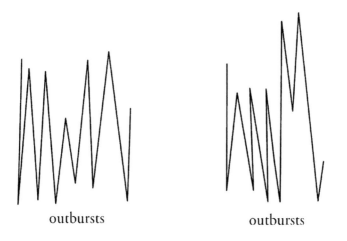

or the flat line of the silence, which gives the illusion of no feelings. We mistake this tension-filled silence for stillness.

---

silence

Given these two choices, most of us would take the flat line of no feeling. So this flat line becomes our goal. We decide we don't want the insanity; we want the choice of NO FEELINGS.

If you think about the monitors attached to patients in the intensive care unit, the first diagram is just before death. The flat line IS death.

A healthy heart makes a pattern like this . . .

This is the rhythm of a healthy heart. It is also the rhythm of a healthy *feeling life.*

Questions to contemplate . . .

How much tolerance do you have for your own feelings— or anyone else's feelings?

How comfortable are you at expressing your feelings?

A simple test:

To measure your tolerance for feelings, pay attention to what happens in your belly, your neck and shoulders, and your chest when someone near you is expressing their feelings. What happens inside your body when you are in the presence of someone expressing fear, hurt, sadness, or grief? Notice your judgments. Do they make you anxious? Do you want them to stop? Just take note.

(Of course, I am not suggesting you hang around for inappropriate expressions of feelings, such as violence.)

Chapter 11:

Our War on Painful Feelings

"Stop crying or I'll give you something to cry about!"
-Source Unknown

Before we can effectively parent, we must first understand the ramifications of how we were parented, and how all of the craziness we grew up in landed on us. Even though craziness is on a continuum, many of us who grew up in crazy families have much in common.

Regardless of how different our external circumstances may be, we share a common internal experience. In other words, it doesn't matter if we are rich or poor, male or female, married or single, or earn our living by our hands or our minds. We share the same childhood experience of not having our needs met and not having our feelings validated. We grew up in family environments that did not feel safe. We didn't feel supported to be all that we could be. Much of the time, our parents' needs overshadowed what we needed. Our parents could not look at their own feelings—consequently they couldn't help us to develop ours. Crazy families operate under three common rules:

1) DON'T TALK: The adults don't talk about what is happening in the family.

2) DON'T TRUST: Because we don't talk, we are not able to trust our feelings. Nothing is identified. Everything is suspect.

3) DON'T FEEL: Our feelings are our key to reality. If that reality is too painful to endure, we shut out our feelings. As youngsters, we can't do the painful feelings alone.

Healthy families understand and expect life to challenge them with problems. Healthy families know how to identify and communicate problems, situations, issues, and their associated feelings. They don't hide from problems and feelings. They discuss problems with the goal of understanding and finding workable solutions. Healthy families understand that feelings offer information. They understand that our feelings offer us insight. Feelings let us know how our experiences have impacted us.

As children, many of us were commanded not to feel. For example, we were scolded, "Stop crying or I'll give you something to cry about." Think about it. When you were a little munchkin, and were threatened or hurt, you spontaneously cried. You were expressing your reality. But your parents insisted that you didn't have a reason to cry.

Or maybe there were times when your parents weren't speaking to each other. While tension permeated the house, no one explained why. The adults insisted that nothing was wrong. Their actions said otherwise. Your whole body and intuition vibrated with red alerts. "Emergency!" your instincts screamed. "Something is wrong here."

Mom, Dad, and older siblings are the gods in a young child's world. Young children want to please the gods. Children instinctively know that they are completely dependent on their caregivers. It is a matter of survival. Young children strive to make Mom and Dad happy. Consequently, if you are trying to please parents who will not let you have your reality, then your only choice is to change your reality. Crazy families are crazy making.

With no explanation, validation, or permission from the adults in your world to feel your feelings, what were your options? You weren't allowed to believe what your "feelings" were telling you. In order to protect yourself, to not rock the boat, you were forced to deny or repress your feelings. You had to convince yourself that you must be mistaken. Instead of feeling, you had to disconnect.

Nature, in her infinite wisdom, gave human beings the ability to block painful feelings. This gift is called denial. She gave us denial as a temporary measure. She didn't mean for us to disconnect from our feelings forever. Nor did she intend we get a free pass and not have our feelings at all. No, that was not her plan. Her plan was to cut us some slack, give us the opportunity to be stronger, older, wiser, or just not so vulnerable, when we finally got around to experiencing our feelings.

How does denial work? Let me explain how it worked for you and me when we were kids. Please note that it works this same way for our children. For this part of the book, however, stay focused on what happened to you as a kid. Try not to go into what you did to your kids and how they might use their own denial. We will get there soon enough.

Denial is practiced one experience at a time. Layer upon layer is built. You learn to anchor your hurtful stories (experiences) down deep. You bury alive the painful reality of your unmet childhood needs. You learn to disconnect. The process of denial becomes habitual and serves to separate you from your experiences. It is as if you took a long and scenic trip with your eyes closed.

This disconnecting, or numbing out, protected you. It helped you to manage the inconsistency between what your feelings were telling you and what your parents were insisting was reality.

Parents in crazy families can't teach what they don't know. Consequently, they teach by default. Their behaviors, more than their words, influence us. Quickly, you learn the rules. Your feelings were not to be honored or validated.

In order for an adult to teach a child about feelings, he or she must be willing to experience his or her own feelings. Without willingness, parents can't teach a child to label and know feelings. Their behavior is teaching avoidance of feelings, or as in the case of raging parents, ones who demonstrate inappropriate outbursts, their behavior is teaching that feelings cannot be controlled.

Crazy families don't communicate. Life in crazy families is black and white. Responses are not appropriate. Problems are ignored or turned into high drama. Either no one is in charge, or one person rules like a dictator. Chaos or silence is the norm. There is terminal seriousness. Compulsive behaviors are often used to cover pain. Behaviors such as overeating, overdrinking, overspending, or turning a small situation into a crisis are the rule. Often the boundaries, the limits, are inappropriate. The boundaries are either non-existent or rigid. Kids are left to make sense out of the inconsistencies. Feelings are avoided and not discussed.

To survive our crazy families, we had to use denial. So much so that we confused our state of denial with reality. It became our default. Eventually, without our permission, denial began dictating our responses to life. Ultimately, we turned away from ourselves. We learned to not trust ourselves. We looked outside of ourselves for our clues, for our information. We lived believing that someone or something else knew what was best for us. We disconnected.

Learning to identify feelings is a fundamental need of all children. The ability to label feelings is as valuable a life skill as learning language. Both should be taught simultaneously. Parents have the primary responsibility of teaching children these skills. It is a process that needs to begin when children are young and evolve over a lifetime.

I want to teach you to recognize the different ways you can practice denial. Learning to label what I was feeling led me to becoming conscious of what I was doing. Without these skills, I would still be on the treadmill of doing what I always did and getting what I always got, which wasn't what I wanted.

It would be easy to teach a child how to identify her feelings if we could point to something concrete, like we can when we teach her to recognize her own foot or hand. We can touch the hand or the foot. We then instruct the child to touch her own hand or foot. All the time we are saying the words… "Hand" and "Foot." The child gets a lot of support reinforcing the words for hand and foot. With all of this repetition, the child then assimilates into her awareness the experience of having hands and feet. This is obviously much simpler than teaching a child an abstract concept like recognizing feelings.

When parents are teaching a child about feelings, they have nothing to point to. They can only suggest or guess at what a child might be feeling with something like, "It looks to me like you are really sad," or, "If that happened to me, I would be angry." In order for an adult to teach a child about feelings, that adult must be able to experience and label his or her own feelings. Crazy families are crazy because feelings are ignored—not acknowledged and not discussed.

An example: Dad comes home late. He has stayed after work with friends and had too much to drink. He diverts attention from his own behavior by getting angry with Mom because he claims dinner is dried out. Mom cries and says that it has been on the stove too long waiting for him, and she reminds him he is three hours late. The kids are sent to bed, and Mom is heard crying at the table while dad is passed out snoring in front of the TV. The next morning at breakfast, Dad kisses Mom goodbye and goes off to work. Mom asks the kids what they want for school lunch. No one talks about last night's drama. No one says, "How are you kids doing? Do you have any questions about last night? I'm sorry that you had to hear all that. I was wondering if we scared you with our anger?" The echoes of the night before lie heavy in the air over the kitchen table, but no one is talking about it. And this isn't the first time a scene like the one the previous night has been played out.

Early on, a child in this family learns not to ask questions such as, "Mom, are you and Dad okay? Are you going to get a divorce?" If they were asked, Mom would snap back with an agitated voice, "Why would you ask such a question? We're just fine. Now eat your breakfast or you'll be late for school."

The unwritten fundamental rule in crazy families—we don't talk about the uncomfortable. We don't talk about our feelings.

So what do children do with the experience? First, they learn not to ask questions. Second, they learn not to trust their own feelings or their interpretations of an experience. In this example, the child experienced the scene of the night before as threatening. It looked and felt to him that Mom and Dad were fighting, and that things at their house were not safe. But Mom, the god of this child's world, has told him everything is fine. She acted as if the question he asked was completely out of line. Thus the child's only left with one choice—to convince himself that he must be wrong. Mom affirms that his feelings are wrong because she has declared another reality. When she says everything is fine, he learns not to trust his own intuition.

From a very young age, children instinctively know that that their well-being is completely dependent upon their primary caregivers. It is basic human nature to survive. From early in our development, human beings realize that we can't make it on our own. We know we need Mommy and Daddy. This is why we change our reality to please them. It is possible to change our thinking, while we are powerless to change their behavior. This is all accomplished subconsciously.

Have you ever been at the grocery store or the mall and seen a small child, three or four years old, who is separated from his or her parents? You may even be able to see the parents frantically moving towards the hysterical child. But in the meantime, there is absolutely no consoling that child. As long as the child can't see Mom and Dad, he or she is hysterical.

The lost child is terrified. In those few moments, for all that child knows, he might as well be looking into the face of death. This is why young children will scream and holler and fight with all their might not to be separated from their parents, even if those same parents are abusive.

In my first teaching position, I worked as head teacher in a pre-school for special needs kids. Daily, I had to observe children for visible signs of physical abuse. One of my most difficult cases was a set of three-year-old twins, a little boy and girl, on whom, more than once, I found cigarette burns. The day finally came when the social workers had to go into the home and take custody away from the parents. The twins fought, screamed, and cried to stay with their Mom and Dad. These parents were the people who were burning the twins as a form of discipline. As difficult as family life was for the twins, these were the parents that they knew.

Young children are not capable of understanding or accepting, "Oh, my parents are inadequate, therefore, I'm in danger. I'm in big trouble." To take in the psychological ramifications of what it means to have parents who are not able to meet your needs, or keep you safe, is much too emotionally devastating for a young child. Heck, many of us as adults still can't accept our parents are not who we need them to be. As such, we continue to practice denial.

A question to contemplate . . .

What did your parents teach you about feelings?

Chapter 12:

Denial Comes in Four Flavors

When I can label my behavior, I own my behavior and then my behavior stops owning me.

Ok, so we use denial as a tool when we are threatened. It is a subconscious act on our part. We default to it, the way we default to holding our breath when we are frightened. We don't have to think about it. We just do it.

Denial is an automatic behavior that keeps us from feeling those deep feelings that we fear are too overwhelming to feel at the time of the experience. When we grow up in crazy families, we get a lot of opportunity to practice denial because we are bombarded with many scary and confusing feelings. Some children were forced to practice denial so frequently that disconnecting and splitting off became their normal behavior. As adults, separation from their core becomes their norm. Sadly, these same adults have no idea how separated they are.

Denial causes us to lose touch with who we really are. It is as though we live in a large house, but we have locked so many doors to so many of the rooms that we have little space for living. The first step to reopening the doors is to recognize the behaviors that no longer serve us. I am speaking about the behaviors that we developed in order not to feel our feelings—the feelings that we believed were too overwhelming.

Our denial behaviors are like a heavy coat that we needed in the winter of our lives, but now it is summer, and we still have the coat on. We are bundled up as if in a straight jacket. Consequently, as adults, many of us are restrained, not able to fully engage life, and have no idea why. We feel like observers in our own lives. We are vague about who we really are, and what we want. A heart that has been hardened from yesterday's pain has difficulty opening for today's joy. We need to stop taking this trip called life with our eyes shut and our hearts locked up.

The overcoat served us well, but we no longer need survival defense mechanisms. We need to recognize we have the coat on. Then we must choose to take it off. We also need to open all of the doors in our "emotional house" and live fully in every one of our rooms.

What does denial look like? And how can we recognize it? Here are some clues.

For teaching purposes I divide denial into four types. They are:

Minimizing, Diversion, Anger, and Refusal

Minimizing. This type of denial is my personal favorite. When we utilize minimizing, we don't deny that things happened. Rather, we just declare we weren't affected. We use phrases such as *I don't care; it wasn't that big a deal;* or *it doesn't bother me.* Essentially, we disregard the magnitude of our own experience.

Minimizing is actually a form of abandonment. We do this in a most profound way. What we are doing when we practice minimizing is telling ourselves that what we experienced didn't matter, didn't count. We can empathize with others and their experiences; we are just not able to do the same for ourselves. It is a diminishing of self by keeping the focus on others.

I grew up being encouraged to focus on how much worse others had it. "What are you complaining about? Look at the starving children in China." There is merit to having awareness of others, but like everything else, it needs to be practiced in moderation. I was taught not to have a self—just to be present for others. The reality is that there will always be someone much worse off than we are. And just as true, there will always be someone who is in a better place. Life is on a continuum. In order to have a real self, we need to know where we are on the continuum and learn to respect our place on that continuum.

We need to deal with where we are at any given time. We can only heal that which is ours. All forms of denial are defense mechanisms, devised to keep us out of our present situation when we want to avoid our current reality. Denial is a survival mechanism given to us to use when we sense danger. Our instinct for survival is primary. Once we have the basic necessities such as water, air, food, shelter, and safety from harm, we are then free to move on to satisfy our more complex needs, like finding meaning and joy in our lives. When we have grown up in a crazy family environment, it is difficult to trust, to take off the coat, to let our guard down. We get stuck in the survival mode. We become so good at protecting ourselves that we don't know how to just be ourselves.

Denial is a process by which we bury our painful feelings as the experience is happening. The emotional pain is shut off and locked in. It is buried alive within us. It doesn't go away until we open the door of our secret hiding places and release it. Old pain is released through feeling. Holding the feelings back wastes much of our good life energy—energy that is not available for joy. No matter what form of denial we use, our valuable life force is depleted.

Some years ago, I was a participant in a co-ed therapy group. Our leader was a male therapist whom I trusted. During one of our sessions, two of the male participants became angry at each other. They were pushing each other's buttons as the tension built. Most of the other eight group members were squirming in their seats and staring at their feet, feeling very uncomfortable with the rising tension. I felt safe and secure that the group leader would handle the situation in such a way that it would be a win/win for everyone.

I sat on the carpeted floor, my arms wrapped around my knees, pulling them into my chest. I watched with wonder as my therapist handled the situation. Each man learned what was his to learn, and the group was returned back to normal. I felt satisfied and comforted. I enjoyed watching the conflict successfully resolved.

My ride home was about an hour long. Fifteen minutes into the ride, I began to cry. I cried from a depth I had long forgotten. I cried so hard that I had to pull off into a rest area because my tears blinded me. Initially, I was puzzled. What was this all about? And then it dawned on me: I was grieving the loss of never having a safe dad. What I had just experienced in my group simulated the feeling of being in a family with a safe dad—a dad who protected the family, who was smart and kind and sober, and who respectfully honored each person, a man who led the group from tension to resolution to comfort.

I have told you that my dad left when I was three years old, and I have not seen him since. I have never heard from him or any of his relatives. My war cry from the time I was an adolescent was, "You don't miss what you don't have." I repeated this sentence whenever anyone would comment how sad it was that I didn't know my father. I completely minimized my loss. I had myself convinced that I didn't miss him. For a very long time, I believed that my dad's absence made no difference to me. I was in complete denial.

For a few moments in the family-like setting of the group, I was able to feel what it would have been like to have a safe dad. That experience dramatically colored the large void that was in my heart. Because of the trust I had in my therapist, I was able to open my heart in the group. I felt warm appreciation for what my therapist did and how lovingly he did it. With my heart wide open, I could feel the void. It needed to be felt. In that surrender, I owned, and was able to release, the feelings of grief, hurt, and sadness that had been locked away for years.

After this revelation, there was an emotional and personal softening in me. I stopped projecting my old anger onto the men in my world. My present husband can vouch for this. Before this group therapy session, he would often remind me, "Irene, I'm on your side." He needed me to put my anger and hurt where it belonged—in my history.

The second type of denial, Diversion, is so accepted in our culture that we see it as an asset. Americans prize busyness. We honor multi-tasking. We get very excited about high productivity. We pump up with caffeine to keep ourselves charged, and we brag about how little sleep we can survive on. Diversion, in the form of busyness, is a very seductive denial choice for many of us who grew up in crazy families. Those of us who have built our personalities around being a human *doing* rather than a human *being* are well supported by our culture.

Diversion, as a form of denial, is basically any behavior that we do in excess, allowing us to keep the focus off of ourselves. We continually are moving, running, and doing, so that we don't have to sit still with our feelings. We work (volunteer or paid). We keep our lives full of other people and their issues. We make a joke out of everything. We pay much too much attention to food, shopping or gambling. We use alcohol or drugs, pornography and sex to keep our attention diverted. We focus on others by blaming or judging. We get lost in books or exercise. We go faster and faster with larger and larger agendas. We numb out with anything that will keep us from feeling, from being present with ourselves.

We have kept this pace for so long that we believe we have no choice. We believe that life lived full speed ahead, with no time for breathing or sitting still, is just the way it is. Anyone who might suggest we slow down is met with our irritation and raised eyebrows. We can't understand their ignorance. *Don't they know how much we have to do, how busy we are, if we don't do it who will, my drinking is my business, it's my money I'll spend what I want.* We have a list of responses. We defend our intense behavior.

Only you can decide if any aspect of your behavior is excessive or out of control. I can't tell you, nor do I want to. I had enough difficulty recognizing how out of control my own work addiction and drinking had become. I encourage you to ask yourself some questions. For instance:

1) Has anyone you loved ever talked to you, with concern, about your drinking, spending, gambling, or use of drugs (prescription or illicit)?

2)   Has anyone you loved ever asked you to sit with them, be with them, or spend some quality time with them, and you could never quite make it happen?

3)   Do you carry around a sense of impending doom, like the other shoe is going to drop at any moment?

4)   Do you ever have the feeling in the midst of all your activity or amid all your possessions of "is this all there is?"

5)   Do you walk around with a sense of incompleteness?

If you can identify with any of the above list, you might want to ask yourself what you are running from. What is nipping at your heels? And then you might want to sit still with it for five minutes. Stop—don't give me, "I have no time." Take it! Take the time. Time is another word for life. It is your life, your time—take it. What are you running from?

Let yourself write about it. Just use a couple of pieces of unlined paper and write yourself a letter. Talk to yourself about your activities, your pace. Ask yourself about your satisfaction level with life. I am not asking why you are running. I am asking you to look at what you are running from. Ask the knot in your stomach, what does it want you to know? This is journaling—not real complicated. I began writing to myself about twenty years ago. It has been the single most effective tool I have used to find my way back to me.

Once you begin to stop, then you need to listen. You know what the simplest form of meditation is? It is breathing. Simply stop and breathe. Focus on your breath for just one moment. You need to listen before some disease or illness forces you to stop. Nature will get your attention one way or the other. When all else fails, our bodies will do what they have to do to get our attention. Life wants us to know our own stories and how those stories landed on us. What meaning did we give our stories? Our stories are our experiences. Without knowing what meaning we have given our experiences, we are not able to know why we are here on the planet.

Anger in the form of denial is when we get mad instead of getting real. We rage at God, at life, at the government, at our neighbors, at other drivers, at our spouses or ex-spouses, at our children, and at ourselves (depression). Our hostility may not be loud or look like rage. We may practice silent hostility i.e. silent violence; we may be full of judgment and criticism, or imagining revenge and punishments. We are quick to judge everything around us. Nothing meets our expectations. We are irritable and bitter. People who love us look at us with frustration. They urge us to lighten up.

We use our energy to stay in our heads. Resentment literally means to re-feel. We hang out in our heads, rehashing old hurts and abuses. We see ourselves as victims. While we are hanging out in our heads with anger, we are separated from our hearts. Each judgment and bitter thought is a brick we add to our walls—walls that lock others out, our children included. Sadly these same walls also lock us in—alone.

Refusal as denial is practiced when we just say no to painful experiences. We pretend they didn't happen until we believe our own deception. We shut out reality completely. We click off. We can block out small or large amounts of our experiences. We do this by disconnecting from our bodies, which is the seat of our feelings. A simple test to see if you are living disconnected from your body—inhale—notice how deep your breath goes. Do you fill your lungs nice and fully or is your breathing shallow? You should be comfortable with it going right down into your belly.

Many adults don't realize they have blocked out childhood experiences. What they do notice is that they don't have as much memory of childhood as their friends do. Often, I will ask a new client, "Do you ever wonder why other people remember more of their childhood than you remember of yours?" Some look at me surprised that I would know to ask them that question. They have been mystified as to why others have so much more access to memory and details about childhood experiences than they do. Lack of memory is a red flag.

Of course, the average adult will have trouble remembering some aspects of their younger years. What I am talking about, in this example, are memory lapses of years. If you can't remember the whole of one, two, or more of your elementary school years, and you know that you grew up in a crazy family, then we are most likely talking denial.

We know that young children have no power against adults. They are at the mercy of their parents. They can't escape adults who are causing them harm. Their only defense is to disconnect from themselves. Split off. We all experience the phenomenon of splitting off at some time or other in our lives. We do it whenever we are faced with a devastating reality we don't want to accept, like the death of a loved one, the loss of a good paying job, or a cancer diagnosis. We are in shock. Shock is a form of denial. We temporarily split off.

A temporary split could look like this: You hear the news that an important loved one has just died. Your whole body rejects the news. All your brain can say is no way—this just can't be true. You can feel yourself flinch. You might even gesture with your hands, pushing away the air in front of you, as if to shield yourself from the news. You find it impossible to wrap your brain around the reality. Nature gives you this shock, this denial, this temporary slack, so that you can adjust. This bit of grace allows you time to take the news in slowly.

You attend the funeral and visit with other family and friends. You relive old memories, maybe even laugh and joke about the loved one. Nothing is real yet.

And then sometime after the funeral is over, when you reach for the phone and you remember your loved one can't be called, or a holiday comes and goes and they are not there—you begin to get it. The reality of the death breaks through the denial and seeps into your consciousness. It must, because this state of shock, this denial, is only meant to be temporary. Without consciousness, without reality, we are not able to function effectively.

On the other hand, a child who is being hurt or abused on a regular basis has no choice but to stay split off in order to survive. The separation for them is more than temporary. This state of disconnectedness is difficult to explain in just a few sentences because all mental health conditions are on a continuum. "Split off" can be as severe as a diagnosis of multiple personality disorder or as simple, but still distressful, as not being able to let love in or out. You know that something inside of you is blocked.

Even though I have divided denial into four categories, most of the time denial is experienced as some combination of the four. However, we do seem to have a tendency towards one more than the others. My hope for you, from this chapter, is that you begin to gain a consciousness of your own behavior. By listening to your thoughts and words, I want you to see if you identify with any of the illustrations. Now, here are some ways to experience and work with denial. Much of what causes us to practice denial are feelings of fear, sadness, hurt, or all three.

Remember anger is always attached to either fear or sadness and hurt.

I am not saying that anger is not a real feeling, but it is a secondary feeling, always linked to either, fear, sadness and hurt, or all three.

To finish or complete our old anger, we must feel the underlying (often-denied) primary feelings. We must feel all of the feelings that are attached to our anger. We need to feel our fear, sadness, and hurt. Resentment keeps us in the rage and out of our heart spaces. It gives us an illusion of power. When we drop into our heart space, we will feel the underlying sadness and hurt or fear that has been buried. These primary feelings leave us vulnerable. Many of us run from that vulnerability. As children growing up in crazy households, we were constantly vulnerable. We avoided the feeling of vulnerability by putting up a defense of anger.

Vulnerability is not a bad thing if you are living in a safe environment with safe parents. But, if you were living in a crazy environment, you couldn't afford vulnerability. You had no power. No power as a child meant you were at the mercy of adults, who often were not safe. You were left in a bind. You had feelings that left you vulnerable and no safety to feel them. Feelings are only finished when they are felt. Feelings are energy. They are vibrations. We need to let them move through. As children, we could not allow our feelings through. As adults we can.

Have you ever let yourself have that good cry? A cry so deep and old it pulled you into the fetal position. And then did you let all the sound that needed to flow, come out? And once done, do you remember the feeling of relief, the stillness that followed? Down in the deepest part of your belly, do you remember the freedom, the space that was cleared? That is finishing the feeling.

The opposite can also be necessary. Some of us (often women) hang out in the sadness and don't allow ourselves to do the anger. Our culture, which is often black and white, gives men more permission to do anger and much less permission to do sadness and hurt. On the other hand, our culture gives women more permission to do the hurt and sadness and less permission to do the anger. We even have words for it. An angry woman is a bitch. An angry man is strong, whereas, a sad man or a fearful man is a wimp. A sad or fearful woman is frail.

There are many healthy ways to release anger, such as screaming into a pillow, banging a Wiffle® ball bat on a bed, chopping wood, going to anger retreats and workshops, or working with a good, safe expressive therapist. It is important when releasing anger that you also allow yourself to release the sound that goes with the anger. Give it voice. Asking a safe friend or relative to witness your release can maximize your healing. Their only job is to watch without judgment. Theirs is to hold the space for you, and assure you that you are ok. This can be wonderfully validating.

As little ones, we were not heard. As adults, we can do it differently. Our feelings are meant to let us know how our life experiences are impacting us. We cannot receive the information available from our feelings if we don't feel them. Once felt, we must give our feelings voice so they can be discharged through our bodies and finished. Denial keeps them buried alive.

There are many different degrees of abuse, neglect, and craziness—and there are just as many degrees of denial. No matter what the degree, all of it is healable—able to be healed. What is required is a willingness to make the journey through your heart into your own past. It is there that you will be able to reclaim your whole self. Once you have, you are then able to be present for others—present in a way that allows you to be in relationships without having to dominate or be subordinate.

A question to contemplate . . .

What forms of denial are you good at

Minimizing,

Diversion,

Anger,

or Refusal?

Chapter 13:

Waking Up and Beginning Again

I didn't know what I didn't know.

In 1969, at the age of 23, no one I knew was talking about the influences of a crazy childhood. We didn't have Oprah or Dr. Phil to teach us how our dysfunctional families affected our lives. No one was using words like "my inner child," at least no one I knew. I don't think most of us knew we even had an inner child.

I had no clue that my childhood was pushing me around in my adult life. I was in the grit-your-teeth-don't-ever-admit-your-fear-or-vulnerability school of thought. As a kid, I didn't let anyone know how bad life was at my house. I certainly wasn't talking about my childhood as an adult. Besides, I had too much to do to be wasting my time reliving what happened to me as a kid. The only glimpse I gave anyone into my story was through my sarcastic humor. I would drop a line like, 'We could have a family dinner, as long as we didn't put any sharp instruments on the table.'

I saw myself as a determined, ballsy kinda broad. I only recognized a-rock-falling-on-my-foot kind of pain. Anything else was a bad attitude.

I had no room in my vocabulary for words like "emotional pain." I was wrapped in the attitude of bravado that permeates youth.

I had no delusions about my childhood. I knew it was filled with insanity, which is why I was determined to do things very differently than my mother. I was convinced that I was doing right by my girls. I was sure that they were having a much better childhood than I did. It was better because it was different.

I was like a soldier in a war. He just puts one foot in front of the other and does what he has to do. No way can a foot soldier with a gun or a pilot waiting to drop a bomb allow himself or herself the luxury of seeing the big picture. They can't let themselves own the ramifications of their behavior on other human beings. Their focus is on getting the job done. Soldiers must hang on tight to their belief in the rightness of their mission. Any kind of reflection could take a soldier off course. She might change her mind about the worthiness of the agenda. She might see the fear that underlaid her every action. Like a soldier, my reflections came much later. Like a soldier, I kept marching forward with my eye on the mission, and like many soldiers, at the end of each day I fortified my resolve with my two new best friends—alcohol and tobacco.

Alcohol and I were fast becoming a steady item. I treated myself to "a glass of wine" every evening after work. "Glass of wine" was my euphemism for keep my glass full all night long. I justified my daily drinking. After all, it was only wine, and I deserved it. I was over 21. I had to give myself some way to relax. Who was I hurting? So what if my head might throb a bit in the mornings or I found myself smoking too many cigarettes. It was a small price a gal might have to pay—maybe I might just need to ease up a little, some day.

I used my first husband, Kevin's, relationship with alcohol as an excuse not to look at my own drinking. This would be called diversion. Kevin was my definition of an alcoholic. He was the one with the problem with alcohol. I used it as a reward for a tough job well done.

When Kevin drank, he often blacked out. I didn't. He cracked up cars and got D.U.I. convictions. I didn't. He spent nights in jail because of his drinking. I didn't. He raged and hit people when he drank. I didn't. He didn't pay bills or show up responsibly for the children. I paid bills and I was there 24/7 for the girls.

At 21 years old, I was not ready to see what my relationship with alcohol was costing me. I couldn't. I could only see what it offered me. It gave me anesthesia that blocked my fear. It numbed the fear that I was unwilling or unprepared to own. Remember, in my childhood, I didn't do fear—I did anger. I couldn't go there. Alcohol provided me with a great detour around my fear; it gave me a diversion.

I was 38 years old when I realized that I was a functioning alcoholic. And my alcoholism never did look like Kevin's. I have learned over 22 years of sobriety that our outside behavior is not what defines an alcoholic. Alcoholism is defined from the inside out. It is not about how much you drink or how often you drink, it is about what it does to you.

When I finally did get sober, and no longer had my anesthesia, I found out that I was filled with fear. I might just as well have found out that I was from another planet. It was that much of a surprise. Looking back, I realized I had been living in denial. I had convinced myself that I was fearless. Without alcohol nightly, I was forced to sit with my feelings. The truth I uncovered was that I was full of fear, and had been all along. I learned that fear was a part of the human experience, it was not some deviant behavior, and if I allowed myself to feel my fear, I would not end up in a straight jacket or drooling in a corner. Instead, I would find a freedom I had never known.

As a young mom, I could not let myself look at any of my fears. This would be simple denial. I didn't let the questions come into the light, into my consciousness—questions like *how could I give the girls what they needed? How would I ever finish school? When would I ever have enough money? Would there ever be a man who I could bring into Lynn and Shawn's life? How much longer would my car keep going?*

Like the soldier on the battlefield, I wouldn't look at the big picture. I concentrated on putting one foot in front of the other. My survival buddies were my wine and my work. I took one class after another. I wrote papers. I read my assigned readings. I opened another bottle of Sangria, Chianti, or Rose. I took tests. I met with professors. I worked days at the daycare center. I smoked cigarettes. I dated. And I bathed, hugged, fed, and shuffled my two little girls from daycare to home to parks to friend's houses.

Each individual thing I did was not necessarily unhealthy. It was the pace and intensity at which I was doing them all. I was obsessed with achieving, with succeeding, with getting to somewhere I wasn't yet. I was driven. I kept a to-do list hanging over my head. Move, go, get, do, and run when you can walk, and move when you can sit still. I didn't know my childhood was always just a few feet behind me, chasing me with truths that I was terrified to unwrap.

People that are driven don't hear what is going on inside of them, much less are they able to listen or hear what two little girls might be saying.

Never say never . . . at least not out loud.

My mother married six times. I married twice. The night before I married Kevin, I can remember every intuitive nerve ending I owned sent out alarms. They all sent the same signal—RUN. I wanted to run. I wanted to call the whole show off. How could I; the chicken had been ordered. Sandy's Restaurant and Lounge was ready for us. My girlfriends and sisters each had their red satin dresses and white rabbit fur muffs. We got married February 14th, the day after Valentine's Day.

I can distinctly remember telling myself not to worry. I could make it work. I was that young and that arrogant and that used to denial. I would make it work. I would make a marriage that I was scared to get into—work. I would go through with the ceremony and party because my mom had her heart set on it. I was having the wedding she never had. I was getting the long white dress, the bridesmaids, the Catholic Mass, and the boneless stuffed breast of chicken. I was also getting the alcoholic husband.

I couldn't imagine anything, but "until death do us part." I never, never, never wanted to be a divorced person. Divorced was my mother—not me. Being married to a man who used his fists on his wife was also my mother's story, and then it became mine. So I did end up divorced, which didn't feel quite so bad until I began thinking about getting married again. Nothing says divorce like a second marriage.

A second marriage means you have to show your divorce papers to get your new marriage license. It means your new husband says things like, "I can't wait until we're married longer than you and Kevin were married." And it means that your children are not with their biological father. They are now the stepchildren.

David came into our lives through a mutual friend. He was in Boston doing an internship as a chaplain at the Massachusetts General Hospital. He was in his last year of graduate school. He had taken a year off during grad school to do a residency program at Cornell. So he was 25 years old when he came into my living room and then my life. He had never been married. He had never been out of school. And he had never had a permanent full-time job. He had the kind of part-time jobs that students get when someone else is paying for their education.

Economically, we could have been raised on different planets. I was brought up on planet How-Is-Mom-Gonna-Pay-The-Rent. He lived on planet, Dad-Wears-A-Tie-And-White-Shirt-To-The-Same-Company-For-40-Years-And-Never-Misses-A-Paycheck. David thought he was raised in middle class America. I thought he was raised in wealth. He was right. It was middle class. It was Peoria, Illinois to boot!

Though the outside circumstances of our childhood looked entirely different, David and I had a lot in common. He played the guitar and I sang. We loved sharing a bottle of wine, and a pack of cigarettes, and hours of conversation. We talked about what he was studying in school, the course of the Vietnam war, the plight of the blacks in South Africa, and the way his mother would freak out when she found out he was dating a divorced Catholic woman with two children.

He had been raised an American Baptist and was just months away from becoming an ordained minister in that denomination. David's mother had pictured a wedding for David to a sweet little Protestant girl who would wear white when she marched down the aisle. The only white dress I was going to wear down the aisle would have to have a black hem. I was divorced.

I think part of David's attraction to me was the fact his mother was so against our union. After only a few months of dating we became engaged. I panicked. I wanted to live together, but not get married. I was terrified of going down that road one more time. David, on the other hand, was persistent. He wanted marriage. He didn't care what his parents wanted. He wanted us to be a permanent couple. Besides, the establishment frowned upon an unmarried couple living together in 1971. I knew that no church hiring committee would allow their minister to be "living in sin."

David was committed to the girls and me. He wanted me to finish my education. He wanted us to be a family. It was a lot easier having a partner and much more fun. So on August 21, 1971, I walked down another aisle, only this time it was a Protestant church, I was dressed in yellow, and David played his twelve-string guitar while we sang a song that he had composed for our special day. His mom and dad watched from the front row as we recited vows we had written ourselves. We were pronounced "husband and wife" by one of David's seminary buddies who was performing his first wedding ceremony. Two more of his best friends read original pieces. His mom kept asking his father if the service was legal, while my Catholic friends thought the whole ceremony was "way cool man." They liked that it was casual and short. The shorter the service, the sooner the party in my mom's backyard would begin.

Together we are one; now which one are we—me or you!

David and Kevin were completely opposite. David was an educated man who loved books and learning. He was, and still is, a very gentle man. I don't think David has ever had a fistfight in his life. I, on the other hand, had a temper that looked a lot like Kevin's. I could aptly be described as a hothead. (I'd like to think I have outgrown that description)

Anyway, we were off and running into our new marriage.

Harville Hendrix, author of *Getting the Love You Want*, and one of David's teachers, theorizes that the traits that initially attract us to our partner are the same characteristics that later on frustrate and even repel us. I have noticed, in my work as a therapist, that it takes about three months for couples to move from what Harville refers to as the "Romantic Stage" of the relationship, where we are afloat in the anesthesia of attraction, to the "Power Struggle Stage." In the Power Struggle Stage, we are in a persistent tug of war. We go from the heavenly *together we are one*, to the hellish *now, which one are we —me or you!*

The good news is that there is a third stage of relationship. This one Harville calls the "Conscious Marriage." The bad news is that when you are in the Power Struggle Stage, you are not sure: a) that you won't kill your partner before you get to consciousness, and b) that there are enough years left in your life to ever achieve consciousness.

In the Conscious Marriage Stage, couples have learned to separate what belongs to their history from what is current. They have also learned how to honor the way in which their partner's demands are calling them to growth. For example, David needed me to put down my guns (my anger) and to allow my vulnerability into the marriage. (You can't have intimacy in a marriage, i.e. closeness, without vulnerability.) Vulnerability was the hardest thing for me to give him because of my history, and yet it was what I needed for my development. I needed more access to my softer side. I was out of balance with my masculine, or tough, side.

I, on the other hand, needed David's power. Because of his mother's mental illness, David had power confused with insanity. He was afraid of his power and yet his strength, his healthy power was exactly what he needed to access for his growth and wholeness.

Unfortunately, it was fifteen years before we were introduced to Harville and his Imago Relationship Theory.

In a nutshell (and our shell was pretty nutty), the theory is that we are attracted to our mate because at a subconscious level, they are the image (imago) of one or both of our parents, and they will wound us the way our parents did. And (it gets better) we are attracted to them so that all of our issues (our baggage) can be brought up into the light for healing. The short version is—we push each other's buttons so that they can be fixed.

I may sound flip here with regards to the Imago Relationship Theory, but I have nothing but profound respect and gratitude for the healthy effect it has had on my marriage and the relationships of thousands of other folks.

Back to the story—our house circa 1972–73

I am now in a marriage to a quiet, gentle man (David, who by the way grew up with a hysterical, go-to-the-psych-ward mom). He marries me, a hothead who was abandoned by her dad.

So here is how the beginning of the marriage looked:

1) David, quiet and not able to discuss his feelings, can sometimes become frozen with decision-making.

2) Irene, verbal, sarcastic, and impulsive is quick to make decisions.

3) To David, Irene's exuberance, which he was initially attracted to, later in the marriage, looks and, more importantly, feels like his mom's crazy behavior.

4) To Irene, David's gentleness, which she loved and that initially made her feel safe, later looks and feels like he is wimpy and abandoning her.

So here they are, off and running into marriage and their future. Add to this the denial they have wrapped themselves in during their crazy childhoods. Then splash the relationship with two little girls from a previous marriage. Stir the whole mix with lots of beer, wine, cigarettes, and a little pot, and you now have the much-repeated drama of the *blended American Family.*

Questions to contemplate . . .

What have your relationships taught you about yourself?

Have you been willing to learn the lessons?

SECTION THREE:
DEVELOPING HEALTHY
RELATIONSHIPS

Chapter 14:

The Good Parent Rules

I wanted to be the Waltons . . . only with better appliances.

What did I believe were the rules for the perfect family? Where did I get my ideas? Ok, let's take a look at them.

- A perfect family must have a house—not an apartment—clean always—decorated with warmth— always feels friendly. (Note the adverb "always")

- Like the Waltons—adults should always be available for the kids— always with patience, warmth, and wisdom. Adults are attractive—strong—capable— always meeting the needs of the kids.

- The adults always show up for kids—selflessly. The grandparents live close by or live in the house with the perfect family—like the show *I Remember Mama*, they don't need much money—because they make up for it with lots of love, humor and great food.

- Mama Walton showed me how to be a mom, and the women on TV commercials showed me how to be a perfect homemaker—cleaning, cooking, serving meals, serving snacks, doing laundry, feeding friends, and waiting for Dad every evening with a hot meal ready.

- In the 50s, I was shown what the perfect mom wears while she performed the aforementioned tasks. She was always wearing a dress pulled into a tiny circle at her waist with a belt that matched her high heel shoes. She always wore a ruffled apron and because she was a modern woman, no dishcloth in her hand—always a sponge.

- In the 60s and 70s, my perfect TV moms taught me that it was okay to wear slacks—but everything else was pretty much the same.

- In the 80s, my mentor/TV moms were going to work outside the house before they came home to always be present for their children. They dusted, cleaned, cooked, and washed clothes with the perfect cleaning products. These magical products made it all possible.

- In the 90s, my perfect TV mom is now driving a BMW or SUV to work and has a wonderful lover or husband (it goes with the car). She hands her kids and yuppie husband a toaster pastry as everyone runs out the door. (Too bad I found her when my kids were already grown.)

So now let's add this all up.

- I grew up in a crazy family and used denial as a way to survive. I imagined a perfect family when I grew up, and I committed to never making the same mistakes my mother made.

- TV shows and commercials were showing me exactly how to create the perfect family that I was already imagining, as I denied the crazy family life I was living.

- I found alcohol, cigarettes, and a little speed once in awhile to give me that extra boost the perfect cleaning products might have missed.

- As if I wasn't far enough out on the limb, I kicked God out of my life when I divorced my first husband and my childhood church.

We promised ourselves we would not make the same mistakes our parents made, and for the most part we didn't. Instead, we created new ones.

We don't see the world, as it is—we see the world as we are. We see it through the filter of our own experience. When you grow up in a crazy family, your history or your old story is filled with unmet childhood needs. These unmet needs lap against your heart like water against the bottom of a boat. Our childhood story forms our foundation and our filter.

It is through the filter of our early experiences that we see the world. Until we have owned how our childhood landed on us, and named the assumptions we came away with, our old story will put its own spin on all our relationships. Putting an old spin on our relationships is all well and good, as long as we are aware of what is happening. Believing our reality is the only truth can wreak havoc on our relationships— especially with our children.

I wish it wasn't the case, but I have many examples of ways in which my old story misguided my behavior.

Being the first-born, by third grade I had the most formal education in my family of origin. I had more schooling than my mom. Because Mom had to work long hours outside the house, I inherited many of her chores and obligations for the family. Understandably, Mom often relied on me in ways that were age inappropriate. I longed to have someone who could help me with my homework and with the household responsibilities. I needed an adult, a mom or a dad, who could answer questions. I wanted someone to patiently explain and coach me through experiences like SATs. I wanted a parent who had been to high school and college and who could guide me through my adolescence.

When my girls were in high school, I didn't want them saddled with chores the way I had been at their age. I wanted them to have all the fun they could. I wanted them in extracurricular activities. My desire to give them what I didn't have blinded me. I hate to admit this, but I can remember once staying up almost all night to type a social studies paper for Shawn Mary. I told myself that I was helping her by typing the paper. In reality, I was writing the paper. She had left her assignment to the last minute and I could only see that she needed her sleep. I was constantly there helping, doing, and fixing. An adult was not parenting my daughter. The wounded teenager in me was parenting her. She was being parented with the agenda that I had as a teenager. I was persistently giving her what I earnestly believed she needed, because after all, it was what I needed when I was a girl. Unfortunately, I was not allowing Shawn to experience the consequences of her procrastination. She was being cheated of a valuable life lesson.

My give-them-everything-I-didn't-get plan of parenting began to break down around the time the girls reached fifth grade. Sadly, I didn't connect the flaws in my plan with the push-pull, love-hate relationship dance that began to entangle the girls and me. Repeatedly, I would begin my day by promising myself that I was not going to raise my voice. I promised myself daily to be patient and loving. Rarely did we get through breakfast and off to work and school without my breaking that promise. I found my adolescent daughters impossible to reason with. From my side of the relationship, I saw me knocking myself out for them. I saw me as being a hard-working-devoted mom who deserved appreciation and understanding from them. I saw them as "never" being able to put themselves in my shoes. (Now don't forget this perspective is coming from a woman who spent her childhood trying to make her own mother happy.) I was continually walking around my family hurt and confused. How could it be that as much as I did for them, they could not see what I needed? So, instead of reassessing the situation, I would dig my heels in harder and do more of the same. I would overdo for them and then blow up because they did not show the kind of appreciation I felt I deserved. They instead acted as self-absorbed pre-teens who grew into self-absorbed teens. I had no clue that narcissism is a part of being an adolescent.

Adolescence is a time of development where kids *should* be wrapped up in their own worlds, trying on different ideas and values. It is a time to learn what fits. They need to experience and compare the world of their friends to the world of their family. They should be exploring the world with the same earnestness that they did as toddlers. What they need from us is a safety net. They need reasonable boundaries and mature encouragement. They don't need to be filling their parents unmet childhood needs.

Now don't misunderstand me. I don't believe that it is ever appropriate for parents to accept unacceptable behavior from their kids. But I do believe it is vital that parents learn to identify normal adolescent behavior. I was frustrated with the girls and they found me to be controlling and a great big "duh." After about our zillionth slamming-bedroom-door, or car-door or bathroom-door scene, David decided that we needed some family therapy. I was not thrilled by the prospect of exposing our family dynamics to a complete stranger. I was also not comfortable with the way the girls and I were struggling, so I agreed.

I can't remember much about the session, I can't even remember the therapist's name, but I can clearly remember something Shawn Mary said. When it was her turn to speak, she looked straight into the therapist's eyes and flatly stated, **"My mother does everything for me . . . she doesn't believe in me . . . she thinks I'm not capable of doing anything."** I was stunned. How could she ever believe I thought she was not capable? How could she think I saw her as inadequate in any way? How could she not be anything but grateful that she was given so much freedom to explore and participate in anything that caught her fancy?

I cherished her gifts and talents. I wanted her free to become all that she was meant to be. I wanted her to have all the freedom I never had. I was so blinded by what I longed for as a kid I couldn't see Shawn as a separate human being, an individual with her own story. I couldn't see her needs differently than mine. In retrospect, I vividly see how my history was setting my agenda as a parent. My unmet childhood needs were dictating to me what my daughter needed.

Shawn didn't need what I needed when I was a teenager. She needed what she needed. She didn't have my story. Shawn had a different childhood than I had. Her childhood caused her to have different needs than my childhood caused me; part of what Shawn needed was to realize the consequences of her actions. She needed to explain to her teacher why her paper wasn't done. She needed to have age-appropriate responsibilities to realize a sense of achievement and participation with the family.

I wish I could say this was the only example of laying my agenda of unmet needs on my kids. Unfortunately, at the time of this particular family therapy session (we have had many), I saw my behavior with Shawn around her schoolwork and chores as an isolated problem. I began to change my behavior a bit. What I didn't realize was that my childhood pain was influencing all aspects of my parenting.

I believe that as parents, our unmet needs are also the agenda with which we measure our kids' success, and consequently, our success as parents. If they have, get, and do everything that we wanted to have, get, and do; then they should certainly be happy and grateful—and we most certainly have succeeded.

My friend Donna once shared with me that she had a sign on her refrigerator declaring that she was being the mom she always wanted to have. Before my research, I'd have enthusiastically copied her. I would have rushed home and put one of those signs on my refrigerator. I would have seen it as an affirmation—a goal. I would have used that little note on my refrigerator as a tool to help keep me on track. The goal was always to be a mom different than my mom. Give my kids all I wanted.

It took me twenty more years from that first family therapy session to learn that Shawn and Lynn didn't need me to be the mom I needed—they needed me to be the mom *they* needed.

A question to contemplate . . .

Can you identify your unmet childhood needs?

Do you know what your good-parent rules are?

Chapter 15:

Growing, Growing, Grown

"Just a minute, I'm not ready yet."
- That would be me.

June 1982

Lynn was graduating from high school and I was not ready. I had no idea what ready looked like, but I knew it didn't look like me. I felt an urgency to grab the microphone and call a halt to the production unfolding before my eyes.

The gymnasium floor was covered with a huge gray canvas drop cloth that puckered under the rows of brown metal folding chairs, which were all obediently waiting to be claimed by the families and friends of the graduates. David and I were seated in the front row with other special guests.

David had been asked to give the invocation. This front row position made us look like parents who knew what they were doing; we did not by any stretch of the imagination, feel qualified.

I was not comfortable. At that time in my life, I was still on occasion abusing alcohol and smoking cigarettes. It was too early in the day to

115

let anyone see me open a bottle of wine, and they were not about to let me light up in the gym. I had to sit still and feel.

The school orchestra began playing "Pomp and Circumstance." A sticky panic rattled in my chest and pride filled my heart as I watched the long column of seniors in their white rented caps and gowns enter the gymnasium. Their faces alive with smiles, with cockiness, and shyness, with naiveté and excitement, they filed into the gymnasium. Each graduate-to-be matched with a chair that had been assigned to them at rehearsal the night before.

Some boldly, others more discretely, one by one they searched the crowd to make sure their moms and dads, brothers and sisters, foster parents, and grandparents could see them. There was Lynn. When she knew we could see her, she smiled. I snapped picture after picture on my little camera, urgently trying to hold on to the moment.

I flashed back to sixteen years earlier when Lynn was barely one. She learned to walk early. She would run forward only to stop abruptly, holding on to the edge of some table or chair, wobbling on her little chubby legs. She would then turn her head and torso to make sure I was still behind her and watching.

On that warm day in June of 1982, I was not ready for my oldest child to move out into the world, and I wasn't convinced she was either. For a moment, I could not remember if she could read. I knew I hadn't taught her enough. If this school superintendent saw her bedroom, he would not be including her in the group he referred to as the generation of young men and women who would bring America forward into the future. I wanted a guarantee that she was going to remember her lunch money as she moved the U.S. of A anywhere.

Much too quickly, it was Lynn's turn. The school board president read her name into the microphone, "Lynn Reagan Tomkinson." She was ready. She walked across the stage. The state of Massachusetts agreed she was qualified. (Of course this is the same state that said she was ready to drive at age 16—another qualification I questioned).

As is her way, she marched forward and moved right ahead into her future, looking back only to make sure we were "still there," and we were watching. She released a shy smile as she accepted her diploma. She would soon turn 18 years of age, the age of legal consent. She no longer needed our written permission to do whatever she decided— just our charge card. The beautiful young woman in front of me on the stage was only one year younger than I was when I gave birth to her.

Lynn graduated over twenty years ago. I remember the experience vividly. When I trace back my disappointment about being a parent, I see her graduation as a benchmark.

I didn't feel the way I thought I would feel on Lynn's graduation day. I expected to feel excited and fulfilled. I felt excited. What I did not feel was fulfilled. As a matter of fact, I felt incomplete. It was a day I had looked forward to for a long time. When I was a single mom, I was constantly worried. *How would I feed the girls? How could I find a sitter? Where will I get enough money? What do I do if they are sick? When will I get a break, some time to myself?*

Back then, I would look out into the horizon of the future and think, just get them to their high school graduation and everything will be OK. I related high school graduation to an end point, goal post—a finish line.

High school graduation had been a line of demarcation in my family. I saw it as my pass out of my crazy family. They would not be able to tell me what to do anymore. I would be on my own. My sister Dotty left after graduation and never looked back. My stepsiblings followed suit. We were expected to put on a coat of maturity, independence, and a level of responsibility that my daughter could not relate to.

For Lynn, it meant a great party and gift checks. It also meant going to college where there would be cool guys and more great parties, no curfew, and her mom and dad would not know the half of what she was doing. Freedom to Lynn was spelled very differently than the way I spelled freedom at eighteen. Lynn spelled freedom – c o l l e g e . I spelled freedom g o – a n y w h e r e – j u s t – g e t - a w a y – f r o m – m y – c r a z y – m o m – a n d – I – a m – o n – m y – o w n .

I believed graduation was a passage that marked a new era. It not only marked our lives, but it was supposed to change us substantially, like the way vinegar changes a cucumber into a pickle—there is no going back. In my blue-collar family, high school graduation meant your childhood was over. If you had asked me that day if I believed Lynn's childhood was over, I am not sure what I would have said. I didn't know it at the time, but I was stuck in between two worlds; the blue-collar-barely-make-ends-meet world of my childhood, and the college-educated-professional world in which David and I had raised Lynn and Shawn. I didn't want Lynn to feel she had to run away from us and never look back. We wanted to support her in college.

So what was I looking for? I didn't know. I only knew I wanted to feel better about our relationship. I wanted to feel easier about our interactions. As the mother of two teenage girls, I felt like I was never doing it right—whatever the "it" was.

Everything was easier when the girls were little. Back then, each developmental stage had specific tasks, such as learning to brush their teeth, go potty, walk, run, ride a bike, tie their shoes, learn to talk. (I have no idea why we encouraged talking—just kidding) My responsibility as a parent was simple. I had to keep them fed, sheltered, clothed, and on track with their developmental tasks. All I had to do was love them and teach them whatever skill it was time for them to learn.

At our house, twelve or thirteen candles on a birthday cake meant full out war with Mom and Dad. No longer were we just in our push-pull-love-hate-dance skirmishes; we were now in use-all-weapons-take-no-prisoners battle!

Because both of our children are female, the majority of attacks seem to be with me. (I, of course, did plenty to fuel the fire). It is the same-gender parent that kids are looking to push against as they forge their identity. Had they been boys, I believe David would have been more the target. Kids, in order to develop a self, must define themselves apart from their parents. They do this by declaring war on those same parents. (Doesn't Mother Nature just have the weirdest sense of humor?)

When the girls were adolescents, I was out of my league. My experience as an adolescent was so completely different from theirs. I had no foundation to appreciate the developmental process that they were growing through. I knew that when I was an adolescent, I would have killed to have a mom like me. My "inner teenager" was appalled by their lack of appreciation for what they had. Not so much for the material things that they had. We were by no means wealthy, and I knew they had friends who had more stuff than they did; what was difficult for me to understand, or have any patience with, was their lack of appreciation for the freedom that David and I gave to them.

We supported them every way we knew how. They attended summer camps, had overnights with friends, and had fun family vacations. We drove our kids, and what felt like everyone else's kids, everywhere they wanted to go. We attended their swim meets and ball games. They were given lots of presents for Christmas. I was never allowed to do what they were allowed to do. I was never given what they were given. So why were we fighting? Why could they not get how fortunate they were?

Once my girls reached adolescence, I was out of control. I did not know how to parent. What was I doing? I kept trying to get a handle on it. I gave the job plenty of energy. In fits and starts, I would read the latest book for frazzled parents. I would then return to the battlefield, sure that this time it was going to be different. I was armed with the new answers. I would try to be patient, and then I would lose my patience. My husband and I would work together in our parenting, and then we would fight about our parenting. We would decide to buy things for the girls, and then we would take things away from them. We would punish, we would go easy on them, or we would go crazy with them. We would be hopeful, or we would be hopeless. We would plead with God, or we would be convinced God was a joke with a sick sense of humor.

I did the only thing I knew to do. I did what I heard other parents do. I complained. I cried. I stomped my feet. I prayed. I worried. I took the family to therapy. The therapist kept me. I was indignant. The therapist just didn't get it. She had no idea how hard I had worked to give my kids everything.

Lynn came home late from her rounds of graduation parties. Understandably, she slept in late the following morning. But the sleep-in turned into the late afternoon sleep-in, and she was still not up. She used dishes that she left dirty in the sink, and her room was a mess. NOTHING was different—nothing except my expectations, which were choking me. I could not talk myself out of my disappointment. I couldn't pretend it wasn't there. OK, I'd wait until September. College would begin; things most certainly would be different then.

Now, if you were fortunate enough to be raised by parents who had the necessary wisdom to understand and support your normal adolescent separation process, then you had a model to copy when your kids reached adolescence. You had some firsthand experience to draw upon that gave you insight into this important developmental stage. You had a model. You had a blueprint for being a parent to teenagers.

Unfortunately for my kids and me, I did not have such a model. Mom personalized everything I did as a kid, especially when I was a teenager. She saw my every move as a deliberate act against her. She came from such wounding that she had no idea about healthy boundaries or adolescent developmental stages.

Her only options were to punish inconsistently and inappropriately, to hit, to lay on heavy guilt, or some combination of all three. She would look at us, and in a pained voice, she would ask, "How could you be so mean to your own mother . . . oh if my mother had lived . . . I would never have treated her this way. You are so cruel to your own mother—go and talk to Father Salmon; you need confession."

As I look back on my adolescence, I realize my sisters and I were good kids. We didn't know that. We were given very little leeway or understanding. For the slightest infractions, we received harsh punishments. We came away from our youth with black-and-blue marks all over our self-esteem.

We left our childhood vowing to parent very differently than Mom did. We were going to have great relationships with our kids. We were going to give them freedom and understanding and the support that we had craved as kids. Our kids were going to be glad we were their moms.

I wanted to do the job right. Being a mom was important to me. No, the truth was I wanted to do the job perfectly. I was far from perfect. Most of the time, I felt I was below adequate. I was frustrated. The girls and I were always fighting. They were pushing limits and arguing with me at every turn. I flipped back and forth from being mad at myself, to being mad at my girls, to being mad at God. What was I doing wrong? What was wrong with Lynn and Shawn? Didn't they get what a great mom they had? I had made their high school lives so much better than mine was "when I was their age." Why couldn't they be more grateful?

They were not more grateful because they weren't me. They had a different life. Their experience of adolescence was different than mine. Their early childhood experience was also different than mine. As far as they were concerned, their mom, me, was just as big a pain in their butts as their grandmother was in mine. They just had different complaints. Whenever the girls and I were arguing, and that was much of the time, I felt I was failing. My conviction was that if I were doing my job as the mom correctly, there would be NO fighting.

Any kind of fighting pushed every old button I had, but even so, this didn't stop me from doing plenty of my own screaming and hollering. Every fighting scene would make me feel like a complete failure, like I had let the whole team down.

A question to contemplate . . .

What makes your disappointment surface?

Chapter 16:

Not Just a Glass of Wine

Miracles are merely the translation of denial into truth.
-A Course in Miracles

I thought I had a calorie problem. I didn't know I had a drinking problem. By the time the girls were in the fifth and sixth grade I had become a functioning alcoholic. To me, that meant that while I held down a responsible job, kept our house clean, was finishing my degree in education and maintaining a 3.89 grade point average, paying bills pretty much on time and putting food on the table when it was supposed to be there—I was a daily drinker.

So what was the problem? What was the big deal? The problem was me. I could blow up and throw a temper tantrum at the drop of a pin when someone in my family didn't pick up their mess. I could flip out when company was coming and turn everyone's stomach into a knot while I made the house "presentable." I was staying up, night after night long after my husband and children were in bed, taking "my time." That meant I was watching Johnny Carson's monologue and finishing off a bottle of wine. I prepared for holidays with a trip to the liquor store as well as the grocery store. I made sure that we packed bottles of wine and cans of beer whenever we went on vacation.

I chose restaurants that served alcohol. I never conceived of a party without alcohol. I judged people who served only one bottle of wine at dinner as cheap. When my doctor asked me to fill out a questionnaire as part of a physical exam and one of the questions instructed me to pick either; a) Never drink alcohol, b) Drink 2-3 drinks a month or c) Drink 3 – 5 drinks a week – I lied and checked off B. The truth is that I was drinking 3-5 glasses of wine a night.

I rationalized the questionnaire to be archaic and ridiculously conservative. I was convinced that I was living a sophisticated lifestyle. My wine in the evening was my winding down—my relaxing. Give me a break. I earned it. I wasn't hurting anyone. OK, maybe I had a headache and a brain fog more mornings than not. So what, it was just the price I had to pay the fiddler. I declared my morning hangovers a result of having too few hours in my day. I'd be fine if I had more sleep. I just needed a 26-hour day. It didn't cross my mind to forget Johnny Carson and my California Chardonnay and go to bed. I refused to connect my morning yuck with my drinking.

However, what I could not deny was my weight. The pounds were creeping on and my hands, face, and feet were often swollen. I knew I needed to lose some pounds. I realized the wine I consumed added extra calories. So I tried cutting back on what I ate. Never did I think about drinking less. Needless to say, my diet plan didn't work. The pounds kept adding up.

At the same time, a neighborhood friend was beginning to look really good. She was dropping weight regularly and glowing with a newfound confidence. I wanted to know her secret. She shared with me that she was going to a twelve-step program called Overeaters Anonymous. I had never heard of either the twelve steps or OA. She invited me to a meeting and said it was free. I figured why not. At the time, I had no idea what a significant life-altering decision that would prove to be.

OA is based on the same twelve steps of recovery, as is Alcoholics Anonymous. The twelve-step philosophy turned my thinking around, which eventually turned my life around. I was introduced to the idea that religion and spirituality were different. I was offered the idea of a Higher Power. At that time, I needed another word for God. I was still angry with God. It was suggested that I not accept anyone else's definition of God but rather decide for myself what my Higher Power was or was not. I quickly recognized that I had God and my childhood religion completely enameled. I had God as my religion and my religion was God.

Many women who are in OA are also in AA. I absorbed their stories as they shared their experience, strength, and hope. They not only shared their experiences with food, but also with alcohol and drugs. I stopped using Kevin's drinking as my definition of alcoholism. I began to identify with these women. I also recognized that as long as I pointed the finger at Kevin and saw him as the alcoholic, I never had to look at my own relationship with alcohol.

I needed to hear phrases like "high bottom drunk." This meant an alcoholic didn't have to end up under a bridge drinking from a bottle in a brown paper bag. That is late-stage alcoholism. Alcoholism or addiction is a disease because it fits the definition of disease. It is progressive and chronic, and left untreated, it will kill.

I began attending the OA meetings faithfully. I didn't speak. I just listened. This in itself was new behavior for me. I had rarely approached anything in my life with the willingness and openness with which I approached those OA meetings. I was able to start looking at my behavior from a new perspective. I saw how I had made alcohol and work my Higher Power. I began to recognize the inherent limits in both.

My introduction to the twelve steps and OA was the beginning of my inner journey. My life until that point had been outwardly focused. All of my goals were of the outside world. They were school, education, jobs, houses, cars, the girls' education, retirement plans, health insurance, vacations, and professional associations—achieve, accumulate, collect, obtain, and arrive. I was running as fast as I could from anything that resembled my childhood.

There is no doubt that what I just listed is important stuff, and we all need much of it. I am also grateful for all the material things I have. But a healthy life is a life lived in balance, and my life was completely out of balance. I had no inner life. I was afraid of what was inside of me.

I am not sharing my twelve-step journey because I believe you or anyone else needs the twelve steps. What I hope you do take away from this chapter is the idea that to heal your wounds from the past, you must go inside. It is an internal job. The twelve-steps was my path inward. You need to find yours. Your path could be a book, a journaling class, a therapist, a course, a group, a church, a meditation class, yoga, Alcoholics Anonymous, Al-Anon, Co-Dependents Anonymous, Adult Children of Alcoholics, one of my workshops—anything that will support you in coming home to your self with honesty and compassion. The inward journey is a trip past our egos, past our defenses, beyond our denial, and right through the middle of our fear. Until we come home to ourselves—come home to the truth of who we have been and who we are—we cannot know ourselves.

We can't make this journey alone. We need guidance and the help of others. Alone, we stay locked in our old way of thinking; we stay stuck in our familiar behaviors. Once you open yourself up with willingness, the right teachers will make themselves known to you; you just need to bring willingness—the willingness to give other ways of thinking a try.

If I don't know me, I can't know you. If I don't know who I am, I can't like me. If I can't like me, then I can't like you; it doesn't matter that you may be my daughter, my husband or my grandchild. I have nothing to offer or give if I don't have me. Practicing denial in any form always works to keep us separated from ourselves.

Questions to contemplate . . .

How do you feel about yourself . . . not what do you think about yourself . . . but how do you feel about yourself?

Do you have compassion for yourself?

Do you feel kindness or gratitude for yourself?

Try this . . . \ . . .

Imagine bringing your five-year-old self out of your history right into your life now. Imagine the child sitting down beside you wherever you are in this moment and time. Ask him/her how he/she feels about who you have become. How does your "younger self" feel about the adult you are today? What are the first thoughts that come to mind? Do the same thing with your "teenage self." Do "these children" feel safe enough to talk to you, or are they feeling your judgment? Just notice.

Chapter 17:

Keeping the Children Safe

We swore we would not make the same mistakes our parents made...
And for the most part we didn't. We created new ones.

It was my favorite holiday—Thanksgiving. I was having my family and some friends for dinner at our house. I was especially excited to be hosting the holiday this particular year because we had just moved into our brand new home, a luxury townhouse. It was the nicest home we had owned. I was looking forward to pulling off a "Martha Stewart" celebration.

The table was set beautifully. David had built a fire in the fireplace. The roasting turkey filled the house with that comforting smell that defines Thanksgiving. Life was good.

There was just one little wrinkle in this perfect picture scene. Both of the girls were late—very late. At the time, Shawn was a senior in high school and Lynn was a college freshman; both were living at home. We knew the girls were together. They had left the night before to attend some kind of homecoming party for kids from their high school who were home for the holiday. This party was the warm-up celebration for the big traditional Thanksgiving Day high school football game.

David and I had not expected them to stay out all night and go to the 10 a.m. game directly from the party. We expected to have seen them sometime before breakfast. This wasn't the first time they had pulled an all-nighter. Neither of us were happy about their behavior, but we were not going to let it ruin the day. We would deal with them later. Since Lynn had started college, we weren't sure what the rules were supposed to be, and Shawn, who was still in high school, was completely convinced she should be allowed to do anything Lynn did.

An hour later, their entrance eliminated any possibility of our family Thanksgiving picture being on the cover of the *Better Homes and Gardens* holiday edition. Both girls arrived disheveled, with bloodshot eyes and obviously hung over. Their blood alcohol content most likely made them legally drunk. Lynn had driven home in that condition. David was furious and we were both embarrassed.

Our company was about to arrive. He yelled at both of them and told them to get out of the house. He didn't want them in the house in their condition. They started to leave but before they got back into the car, I went after them and told them to come back in the house. I was relieved they were alive, and I wanted to choke them both. I also didn't want my turkey to burn, and I wanted my company to feel welcomed. I didn't want to make them uncomfortable watching me kill my daughters.

Once into the house, Lynn wanted to know who was expected for dinner. I told her who was coming, and she insisted I go up to my bedroom with her because she needed to tell me something. The three of us climbed the stairs while David went into the kitchen to finish whatever he was doing to help move dinner along. He was mad at me and I was angry with him. This was a familiar dance we would often do over some struggle with the girls. He saw me as too lenient, and I saw his behavior as shaming. I thought he was building a wall that pushed the girls away. When Shawn reached her bedroom door, she left our little parade and flopped into her bed. She didn't come out for about eighteen hours. Lynn continued leading me to my room. After closing the door, she asked me to please listen. That wasn't an easy request for me to fill. I like to scream and holler when I kill a drunken daughter.

Lynn where have you been?

Mom, just listen.

OK, now tell me what have you been doing?

Mom, why is he coming?

Who?

Him, _____. I thought he was still out to sea.

He had some leave, so he came home to surprise us. What has his coming here have to do with your behavior? And don't raise your voice.

Mom, I hate him and I won't eat at the same table with him.

Lynn, what are you talking about? You're drunk.

I'm not drunk. I know what I'm talking about. He sexually abused me. Twice when I was four years old and you had him baby-sit us. That's when he forced me to _____ ____ ____ __ ___ ____. I was four years old. You let him baby-sit us. I hate him.

What? When? When he was a teenager? He was fourteen—you were four—what are you telling me!?! Why haven't you ever told me this before? Lynn, what are you telling me!?!

SNAP—The world stopped.

She started to shake and cry and shiver. I went numb. She fell on my bed. I held her while she cried. The smell of turkey filled the room even though the door was closed. In moments, she was asleep or passed out. It would be about twelve hours before she came down the stairs. It would be long after the guests had gone home.

I served the meal. I made conversation. I cleaned the kitchen. I made coffee. I played charades. I served dessert. And my mind never left Lynn's bedside. I was completely split. My body went through all the expected motions, while my mind and heart were spinning in a world that had just been flipped upside down like a snow globe. All the pieces were still there, but snow was falling from the ground to the sky.

What do you say to your daughter when she wakes up from sleeping off a drug and alcohol binge after telling you that for fourteen years she has been keeping a huge dark secret from you—that you have been living from a wrong assumption, and because of your wrong assumption you have been misguided in the decisions that you have made for her care and well-being? In a nutshell, with the revelation of her secret, I realized that I had been off base, off the mark, in the wrong line, using the wrong form, bringing home someone else's dry cleaning, missed the train, going in the wrong direction—I HAD BLOWN IT! For years, I was convinced that her problems at school with teachers and principals were all related to my divorcing her father. I had given her divorced parents—the one thing I had pledged never to do—and therefore, I assumed every bump in her social development was a direct result of my divorce. In my guilt and shame about my divorce, I completely missed the mark. Everything was much more complicated than I had ever realized.

And to top it off, I just gave her perpetrator a doggie bag of Thanksgiving leftovers to take back to the base?

What do you say to your daughter?

I said, "Lynn—are you hungry?"

A question to contemplate . . .

What do you know now that you wish you had known then?

Chapter 18:

Crisis Means Turning Point

Be still and know that I am...

-Psalms 46:10

The morning of my little sister's father's funeral, I can remember looking out the window of the black limousine in amazement. Jack, my mother's fourth husband and a man I hated, was dead. I couldn't believe that everything was still the same. People were going to work and school. The traffic lights were blinking red, green, and yellow as always. The superintendent of schools had not declared a no-school day. And I was hungry. We didn't have breakfast because my mom wanted us to receive Communion at Jack's funeral Mass. The rules of the church at that time were no food before taking the Communion wafer. How could it be that the world was just the same as it was the day before Jack died? And yet everything in our family's world was completely different.

I was fifteen years old and it was the first death I had ever been exposed to. It was my first ride in a limousine, my first time standing in a family receiving line at a wake. I was nagged by a feeling that I should be doing, feeling, thinking something different than I was. I felt guilty that I could still want breakfast and that I wasn't crying. I watched my mom collapse in a pile of wailing and screaming hysteria. I just felt like a robot with an appetite.

So let us fast-forward to twenty-three years later. That's how it was when Lynn told me of her abuse. My world was again stopped. I woke up that Friday morning after the *special* Thanksgiving, and I didn't know how to be. I didn't know what I should do, if anything. How do you live your life the next day—the day after a crisis? How do you live your life the day after a life altering "a-ha?" What changes do you make?

We were no longer the same family. I didn't know it at the time, but everything had to change. When Lynn exposed her secret, it was as if she rolled over a large dead log in the middle of our lives, and strange creatures were crawling out everywhere. All of my memories were being reshuffled. Lynn's revelation changed all the scenes in my head. Nothing was how I thought it was; if I was so wrong about Lynn and her behavior, what else have I been wrong about?

This time it wasn't about my mother and her divorces. It wasn't about my stepfathers. It wasn't about growing up in poverty or even about the Catholic Church. This time it was about something that happened to my daughter, that hurt her terribly and of which I had been clueless. It was about how I didn't know what I didn't know, and how I didn't protect her. I hadn't kept her safe. It was about the way my daughter was hurt on my watch. And all of my education and information didn't change a thing. Lynn had been sexually abused and for fourteen years I didn't know. She was also not a little girl anymore. She was eighteen years old.

My new involvement in the twelve-step program was opening me to seeing the world and my place in it differently. We had three issues before us—a) family incest, b) illegal drug use, and c) underage drinking. Initially, I wanted to point the finger at the girls and preach to them about their use and abuse of alcohol, the danger of illegal drugs, and their out of control behavior. I can understand why I wanted to preach. The girls were underage. Their drinking was a problem. Drug use was completely unacceptable. But, it wasn't the only place that my attention needed to go. I needed to own what part of the mess unraveling in our family was mine. It would be a few more months before I would join a second program, and take an honest look at my own drinking.

It was Lynn who turned the conversation on me and said, "Mom why are you drinking?" I defensively screamed back at her that she was not old enough to question my drinking. I couldn't give her or myself a believable answer. I wanted to say because I am old enough and I have a legal right, because it enhances my meals, because I need to relax and drinking is the way I do it—because, because, because.

The real "because" was that it had become my crutch and my God. It was with me all the time. Alcohol was my friend and what I trusted, and I was scared to put it down. Alcohol and my work addiction, all of my motion, kept me from being still with myself.

The family crisis didn't just slow me down; it slammed me into a stop. It stopped me long enough to gift me with a few moments of honesty. Alcohol was a big part of my denial system. My wall of denial was cracked on that Thanksgiving Day. Through the crack, I was able to see how my determination and resentments from my childhood had kept me running. I had been running as fast as I could for all of my adult life. A person can't listen effectively while running. A running mother is not able to pick up clues. She is not able to let go of her own agenda long enough to stop and listen.

How do you live your life the day after a crisis? I only know one way. You live your life one day at a time, and you make the necessary changes one step at a time. I didn't always know that. Earlier in my life, before I began looking at my walls of denial, before I learned to put alcohol down and begin to connect with myself, before I learned that I must allow other people to live their own lives even if I had birthed or married those people, I would have spent that Friday morning on super alert. I would have been in crisis mode—lots of drama. Calling anyone I could think of, who would have recommended anyone they knew, so that I could immediately get my daughter some help, any help. I would have to be doing something. Crisis meant action. Action in those days was another word for reaction of the knee-jerk variety.

I would have gone into overdrive trying to undo the past fourteen years of not knowing, as if that were possible. I would have put all of my energy and focus on Lynn and what she needed and how could I get her help quickly. I would have operated under an assumption that everything must be done immediately. When you grow up in violence the way I did, or any kind of craziness for that matter, crisis is either ignored or means immediate high drama action because someone needs to be protected. But that was my old story. Every crisis isn't the same and doesn't need the same kind of response. Fortunately for our family, I was just beginning to learn that.

At the time, I didn't know what we needed to do, but at least I knew nothing had to be done immediately. I was beginning to see the obvious—like Lynn had been holding this secret for fourteen years and nothing had to be done immediately. She was 18 years old; she had to be involved in choosing her course of action, if any, she wanted to take. How she moved forward was not up to me. My job was to support, not decide.

Slowing down and not reacting was a major change in behavior for me. Being able to pause and not just react is a deciding factor in what separates human beings from the rest of the animal kingdom. I was just beginning to get it. And I was looking at me. I was looking at myself in a way I had never looked at myself before. I was just starting to appreciate the difference between responding to a crisis rather than reacting to it.

With the introduction of the idea that religion and spirituality were separate, I could once again have a relationship with God. I began to see that it was an important rite of passage to develop an adult relationship with the Higher Power of my understanding. In other words, I was a big girl now and it was time to have a big girl's God. I needed to make sense out of the Universe and life for myself. I needed to find the God of my understanding—not what others believed, but what I believed. What was my truth?

The second new idea that I was beginning to assimilate was the concept that God or a Higher Power spoke to me through my intuition. If I were clean and sober, not under the influence of any mind-altering substances like alcohol, and if I allowed myself to be still, then I would be able to connect with the guidance from my intuition. I could hear the still, small voice. This was not the voice of my ego, not the chatter of my willfulness, but rather the quiet and persistent voice from my gut. I was learning that I had all the answers that I needed, if I were willing to listen to the quiet wisdom that had always been with me. I was learning to trust my inner voice—again.

This voice that was present when I was a child—the voice that I had been taught not to trust. The voice that I was forced to shut down, because I was expected to listen to the voices of the adults in my world—adults who had been taught not to listen to their own inner voices.

I was also learning that I only had my answers, I didn't have your answers, and I didn't have my daughters' answers—they each had their own. I could offer them support and encourage them to listen and trust their own inner voices, but the choice was theirs; not mine. This was a big change for us as a family—one that I did not make quickly or smoothly, one that I can still struggle with today. Control was one of my drugs of choice. The amount of control anyone wants is equal to the amount of fear they have—and I had a lot of fear. Much of my fear was old stuff that I had kept in plastic garment bags in the closets of my cellular makeup. It was so familiar it felt like it was welded to my DNA.

Now with Lynn's revelation, I was being confronted with the ramifications of my years of denial. I was on to myself. The gig was up. I was outed. I couldn't lie to myself anymore. It was time for me realize that when you point one finger at someone else, three are pointing back at you. I had been pointing my finger at my mother, my ex-husband, the Catholic Church, and the clergy. Now I needed to look at me. Now conscious of my work addiction, having put down alcohol and pushed by my family to let go of my control issues—I had to start sitting still with me. It was time for me to acknowledge the old agenda created from my old resentments that had been bossing me around for so many years. I had to look at how I had used alcohol with cigarettes and work addiction to feed the fires of my resentments, to keep me from feeling and releasing my old emotional pain.

I can remember the first time I took a mentor's advice and sat down to do one minute of meditation. I literally had the television on, a book propped up in a plastic holder, a cup of tea, and I was knitting. I decided that to meditate I needed to shut off the television. (We are not talking a walking Buddha here.) I called my mentor back and proudly let her know I had sat in meditation for the last minute. A woman wise to my ways, she asked me to describe how I did it. I told her that I had shut off the television and just sat still with my knitting, cup of tea, and book. (I was serious.)

She told me that when she said to sit still, she meant with nothing. She wanted me to sit for one minute with nothing. All I could hear was that she was asking me to waste time. Sitting and doing nothing meant wasting time. Didn't she get how busy I was? How much I had to do? She said if Jesus Christ could slow his schedule down to sit still for a minute, so could I.

Knowing that my way of doing things had helped to get my family into the emotional mess we were in now, I surrendered to her suggestion. Surrendering and becoming teachable, learning to be willing and open, has completely changed my life for the better. I have grown from a person run by self will, who had no idea how to be with herself for one minute, to a woman who cherishes solitude, a woman who today has a working, living, breathing relationship with herself and her Higher Power. These relationships have come to fruition through the practice of being in silence and the stillness.

My introduction to the twelve-step philosophy opened me up to many new paths. I took courses, seminars, spent time with many mentors, and read lots of books, all of which came into my hands just when I needed them. Over and again, my experience has proven that when the student is ready, the teacher will appear. I become the student when I allow myself to be teachable. If I boil down the juice of it all, it is reduced to a simple idea—be still and know. As it instructs in the Scriptures, the way to the kingdom of heaven is to become as a child. A child is innocent and teachable. A child is open and willing. A child is vulnerable.

I interpret the kingdom of heaven as a metaphor for peace and happiness—a peace that is available right here on earth. I have experienced the kingdom in many ways—such as ideas that come in a quiet flash that are beyond my wisdom, behavior that is dramatically different from my crazy normal, or synchronicity that proves to me I am protected. I have experienced the transformation from my fear-based, ego-driven mind to a wisdom instructed by my inner knowing.

I am not saying that I began sitting on a pillow and everything is hunky-dory at our house. No way. We have dealt with all the kind of messy stuff that shows up on Oprah as a topic for her shows. We are a family of live human beings, a family whose roots are planted in some real insanity dusted by colorful genetic challenges. The difference is that today we have a manual. We have a path. And the path takes us to an internal place where we meet the guides of our own understanding. All of us have benefited from twelve-step recovery programs and we each have found spiritual communities that fit our beliefs. Though we differ in the ways we practice our beliefs, we know that our answers lie inside of us, and we are learning to respect and honor each other's choices.

As a child, I had a loyal, innocent, and satisfying relationship with God. For me, God was all mixed up with Jesus and the Virgin Mary. I prayed to each regularly. I often walked three miles to morning Mass to be comforted by them, to love them and to appease them. They gave me the comfort and safety I couldn't find at home. I hung on to my relationship with them like Tom Harks held on to Wilson, his volleyball man, in the movie *Castaway*. They gave me solid ground on which to stand. With them I never felt adrift or alone. Believing in them offered me hope and enabled me to trust life.

So you see, when I stopped doing business with the church because I felt betrayed, I stopped doing business with God and his cast of characters. I saw them all—God, Jesus, Mary, and the Pope—in cahoots together for no good. They were all a part of the Catholic Church, and I felt it had sold me down the river.

From the time I slammed the rectory door shut as a young frightened mother until I understood that religion and spirituality were separate, and God and my childhood church were not the same, I invested all

143

my trust into my own determination and self-will. I took my comfort from my wine. No more was I in relationship with something I couldn't see or touch!

Paradoxically, I can write what I just wrote and know it was true, but also true was the fact that I wanted a church for my girls. And also true was the fact that I married David, who was just graduating from theological school, and was about to become an associate minister to his first congregation. I signed up to be the minister's wife.

In retrospect, I can see that something in me was not finished with God. I didn't see the irony at the time. I didn't see the connection. The Protestant church that David was serving seemed completely different from the church I grew up in. I didn't see it was still about God. The God in this Protestant church felt much more like a political movement, a community meeting, or a neighborhood get-together. The sermons seemed more like talks. The ministers were talking about practicing kindness, and charity, and living peacefully with your neighbor. The topics were filled with sound advice from which to guide your family, but very different dogma than what I was familiar with.

After only two years in the church ministry, David realized it was not the career path he wanted. He left the ministry and moved into social work. Eventually, he and I became psychotherapists. (The joke is that if you are a little sick you go to a therapist. If you are a lot sick you become a therapist!) For years, we continued to church shop. Not as a career path, but as a place to raise our children. Off and on, we tried many different denominations. There was much we liked and much we didn't like. However, as soon as someone would start preaching that they had the only way for everyone, we would move along. The idea of exclusiveness just didn't work for us.

In all the time I was looking for a church, I wasn't acknowledging the depth of the void that I was trying to fill. I was so accustomed to minimizing my needs. I could only recognize that the girls needed the educational experience of a church community. I wasn't able to honor how much I missed God. After a while, we became discouraged; we lost interest in the church search and bought a boat. We spent weekends on the water enjoying nature, celebrating the beautiful world we lived in, and drinking beer. Don't misunderstand me. We had no illusions that the boat was replacing church. It was just what we did on Sundays in the summer. In the winter, we skied.

Once I stopped drinking, it seemed everything began to change. One example of the difference—the girls were becoming independent young women, so they weren't joining us on our Sunday outings as frequently. Our lives were different. Friends with whom we had boated for years dropped us as "playmates" when we weren't drinking anymore. At first, it was difficult to believe life as a family would ever be easy or fun again. We were all looking at our drinking. We each had to look at what we had been substituting for our God. Your God is where you put your trust. Where had we been putting our trust? The girls, each in their own way and in their own time, asked for help and went into a rehab program. They were forging their own paths, finding the tools that worked for them. I was learning to get out of their way. The most challenging thing I do, even today, is to stay out of my daughters' way. When your kids go to rehab, the whole family goes to rehab. We all participated in the family sessions and each of us had to examine our own destructive behaviors. Eventually, David acknowledged his addictions and each of us found the support groups that worked for us. But the single most crucial thread that I see woven through all of our journeys has been the thread that has led each of us to the God of our own understanding. Finding the God of your understanding is the door to your essence. The key to that door is your willingness. Willingness to learn what is ours to learn is what brings us to consciousness.

Once anyone puts down the tools of their denial system, be it anger, food, work, gambling, drugs, spending, controlling behavior, sex— whatever—the void must be filled. These false Gods must be replaced. These old tools have allowed you to build walls that have kept you away from yourself. They have kept you separated you from your core.

Your *core* is the center of you, your essence, the place inside of you that you abandoned as a child in order to survive whatever craziness was going on at your house. Without reconnecting, without coming home to your authentic self, nothing will change. You will continue to do what you have always done—often—just more of it. Without access to your core, you can't find your dreams, you can't find your voice, and you have no real idea who you are and what you are about. You will just get older and your kids will get grayer. But the dance of disappointment and frustration will continue. It will continue until a crisis blows up in the middle of your family and your log rolls over. The crisis can be a major illness, divorce, arrest, one last ugly argument, an affair—the list goes on and on. Maybe it has already happened and that is why you picked up this book.

Questions for reflection . . .

Do you have a God of your own understanding?

How does this God compare to the God of your childhood?

Chapter 19:

Healing Happens

Do the next right thing . . . one step at a time—one day at a time.

The healing process is a tough taskmaster. Healing demands willingness and honesty. The reward is wisdom. Wisdom seems to be a gift of willingness.

A few years ago, Lynn, now a grown woman, lost her home and many of her assets in a nasty divorce settlement. Working hard to make the best of what she considered unfair treatment by the court, she bought a home in a low-income area with the idea of fixing it up and selling it for a profit. In the meantime, she could live there economically.

The first time David and I drove into Lynn's neighborhood and I saw the poorly kept homes, waves of my old childhood shame came oozing up to the surface of my skin. I was no longer in the moment. I was in my history, my old story. I was lost in my childhood, and I was back being the kid from the wrong side of town. I didn't want Lynn to live in that neighborhood or on that street, and I didn't want to be reminded where I had come from by the wave of shame I was feeling. I wanted to turn the car around and find my ex-son-in law and beat him with my fists. I wanted to binge on my rage. I sure as hell didn't want to feel the shame.

The little girl inside of me, who had lived daily with shame, had popped out of my history and was running my show. She might just as well have been driving the car. As a child, I had hopes and dreams for my children to live on a much different street than the street that I was looking at. That vision was a part of my unspoken agenda. Some of our pain-filled experiences were numbed by dreams of a better life for our children. When I was a kid, instead of feeling the shame I experienced because of our poverty, I locked those difficult feelings away somewhere in my subconscious. I diverted myself with dreams of a family of my own. I was going to do things differently than my mother, and give my kids everything I didn't get. I tricked myself into believing those feelings of shame were gone. They weren't gone. Feelings are always buried alive.

I was able to ask David to pull the car over to the side of the road. I then paused. (Remember, the ability to pause and not immediately react is an important skill that separates us from the rest of the animal kingdom.) I had options. I was no longer being held hostage by my history. I was practicing new behavior. I forced myself to breathe deeply, to slow down, and to share with David what I was feeling. I was not running from my shame by fueling it with anger until it was rage.

My old behavior would have been pure reaction. I would have turned my uncomfortable feelings of shame into a blast of blaming. I would have ranted and raved about the courts, my ex-son-in-law, and then finally, I would have finished by being irritated with my daughter for her choices. I would not have been able to see the origin of my feelings. I would not have been able to recognize that the intensity of what I was feeling was a clear signal that I was standing in my history. I would have taken my anger, my wall of denial, and pushed it right into Lynn's new living room.

Instead, with the gift of willingness, I was able to sit with my uncomfortable feelings because now I was able to recognize the source. I allowed the sadness to surface. I didn't run from the pain. I trusted that the emotional pain wouldn't kill me. I trusted that I wasn't going to implode or explode, or both, and end up in some psych ward drooling. I know that sounds like overkill, but we are a nation running from feelings as fast as we can. We are terrified that we are somehow physically and emotionally unequipped to deal with difficult feelings. Today I trust the process of feeling my feelings and then releasing them. What I had long ago buried alive, I now allowed to move into the light, move into the present. Once in the light, once felt, it was completed, it dissipated through the tears. Feeling your feelings is never as bad as your resistance tells you it will be.

David listened while I cried and shared my feelings. They were not right or wrong. They just were. I allowed another piece of my history to be finished. Lynn had once again shown up as my teacher without ever knowing she did. Once in Lynn's home, free of the veil of my history, I was able to experience her enthusiasm and delight with color choices she had made and painting she had finished. She was enjoying a sense of accomplishment. And because I was emotionally present, and not still in my history, I didn't spoil any of her success. The house was her story. The shame was mine. I was able to separate the two.

Today I give my family my continued willingness to own how my childhood landed on me, and how my interpretations of those experiences shaped my life. I have the willingness to separate my history from the present—not by pretending it didn't happen, or walling myself off with alcohol and work so as not to feel it—but by consciously accepting it. Today I am willing to explore my history, so that I can feel it and let it go. Each layer, once felt, each experience honored and acknowledged is a layer that never has to be felt again. More importantly, it is a layer that doesn't get sprayed all over my relationships.

Our childhoods were difficult. That is why they need to be finished. And they can only be finished when we are willing to walk through them, when we are able to own what happened to us. Not like a reporter, sharing from your intellect as if your life were a documentary, but instead, sharing from your experience as the living, breathing, feeling human being that you are. When we own what is ours to own—our feelings along with our thoughts—then and only then are we able to experience release from our stories.

We co-create this healing process by offering our willingness to feel what is ours to feel, which allows us to learn what is ours to learn. When we show up in our lives with willingness, then everything and everyone becomes a teacher, especially our children. Overreactions, obsessions, and controlling behaviors show us that we are stuck in our history. Once unstuck from our history, we are then able to be present in our lives. The present is the only place that joy can be experienced.

Some thoughts for reflection . . .

Think about a time when you faced your history head on.

Chapter 20:

A Daughter's Life

It's the journey . . . not the destination.

January 15, 2003—11:00 a.m.

I am sitting in one of the soft chairs at Barnes and Noble Booksellers. Through a speaker above my head, some Latin singing group is serenading me with a pulsing Salsa sound, while the Espresso steamer hisses in the Starbucks café that is located inside the bookstore. I love to hang out in bookstores.

Shawn Mary is out in the parking lot napping in my car. We are killing time till 4:00 p.m. Killing time—I don't want time dead. I also don't want the fetus in Shawn's uterus to be dead, but it is. We found out yesterday. We saw the lifeless little glob on the screen of the ultrasound machine. An unrelenting flat line unrolled on the bottom of the screen. Shawn looked at me with pleading eyes. I couldn't fix it. I couldn't make the boo boo better. I couldn't bring the baby back.

Between yesterday morning and today everything has changed, and nothing has changed. It all looks the same at Barnes and Noble. But at 4:00 p.m. we will head back to York Hospital, in York, Maine where Shawn will be put under sedation. Dr. Wagoner and Shawn were supposed to be building a relationship, one appointment at a time. These appointments were to be scheduled at two-week intervals, while the fetus inside Shawn was scheduled to grow into a baby, a human being, a grandchild, a personality, a daughter, a student, a friend, a possibility.

3:00 p.m.—Same day

Now I am sitting in the waiting room of Day Surgery at York Hospital. So instead of a regular pre-natal visit with Dr. Wagoner, instead of talking about how many centimeters the baby has grown; we are talking about vacuuming and suction, signing release forms, and a prescription for Tylenol with codeine.

Newborn babies, infants, and toddlers who are having their regular checkups surround us. They are all over this place. I don't want Shawn to hear their cries or laughter. I don't want to witness the longing in her eyes. I want them all gathered up and moved to another part of the hospital.

She is in physical and emotional pain. Dr. Wagoner treated her this morning with some vaginal seaweed (who knew?). The seaweed swells throughout the day and causes Shawn's cervix to dilate. The baby was supposed to cause the dilation, and not for at least another six months. It was not supposed to happen this way. What makes this even more painful is that Shawn was here just fourteen months ago in the exact same scenario. When she came in for her twelve-week check-up, they couldn't find the baby's heartbeat. Both times her pregnancies began very positively—lots of movement and a great heartbeat. And then just a few weeks later, there is nothing—a flat line.

I am watching and listening. I breathe and feel. I stay present. I hold her hand. I listen. I say I love you.

Shawn believes that God/Life/Spirit has a bigger plan and that there is a reason for everything. She is holding on tight to her belief. I am proud of the way Shawn is handling her disappointment. She has cried and cried. Her pain comes over her in waves. Her face contorts with the flush of reality, as it waves over her, and she is forced to embrace the hard truth that this pregnancy is over. She is not bitter. She believes from a deep internal knowing that there is a reason for this miscarriage, and that Life has a plan. In one moment, her face reveals the woman that she is, reflective and thoughtful. Then just as quickly, the harsh reality of her loss breaks through the shock in another unmerciful wave, and I see the hurt, disappointed little girl I have known since her birth.

I watch. She questions me. "Mom, do you think I exercised too much? Mom, do you think it's my age? Why, Mom? People who drink and smoke, they just pop babies out?" And then just as quickly, I hear her say, "Mom, I know that God has a plan for me. I can see myself pregnant and delivering a wonderful baby. It is going to be in God's time, not mine."

I stay present. I want to fix something—anything. I know I can't. I get cups of tea. I hug. I say I love you. I don't question today what is mine to do. Mine today is to be right where I am. I am grateful that I have the freedom to be here with Shawn. I didn't have to ask a boss for the time off. Today, it is clear to me what my job is as the mother of this adult daughter. Mine is to be here to hold the space, to be her witness. Mine is to honor her passage as Life presents her with a challenge. This challenge is between Shawn and Life. Life has a teaching for Shawn through this experience, and it is not mine to do for her. It is hers to do. Mine is to witness and to assure her that she has what it takes to meet the challenge. Mine is to encourage her to feel whatever she is feeling and to know that she is loved and she is lovable. I am able to offer Shawn the wisdom I have gained from twenty more years on the planet than she has. I know from experience that we get through these challenges we are sure we will never survive.

I think about Shawn's birth. How young I was. I think about our journey together as mother and daughter. I think about all the times I have blown it with Shawn. Put my nose into stuff that wasn't my business. I know I offered advice that I am sure sounded like criticism. I remember the social studies paper I typed. I recalled the times I couldn't hear what she was trying to tell me, because everything I heard her say was filtered through my own ideas. I was too absorbed in my need to fix or do, always referencing everything to my old story. My old story was a childhood very different from the childhood that Shawn experienced. It was my childhood, not hers.

Today, I have separated the two. Today, I feel very different. Today, I know where I end and my daughters begin. I am not trying to control anything. I understand. I get it. From the inside of my heart, I know that I am not in control. I am powerless over this chapter in Shawn's life. This is not my story. This is Shawn's story.

I have never experienced a miscarriage. I became pregnant the first time I had intercourse. Within two years, I had two healthy babies. All day long I have remembered that this is Shawn's story. This adult woman in front of me is doing what is hers to do. I don't question that I am only a co-star in this scene. Shawn has been given the lead role. I don't rant and rave. I don't look for someone or something to blame. I don't have a need to change what is happening or to divert myself from the pain of what I am experiencing. I am just being present with what is. Neither of us is practicing denial.

She thanks me for being with her and asks me, "How much is it costing you, Mom, to lose these two days of work?" I let her know that I will see those clients at another time. She falls asleep. She is wiped. I sit with her quietly, just knowing that I am where I am supposed to be, and I have something to offer. I am her mom.

A thought for reflection . . .

Think about a time when you know you did it RIGHT!

Epilogue

The girls are now women with husbands and homes and even one precious little girl. Lynn has a wonderful little girl named Julia. She is the light in the middle of our family. Shawn and her husband have been challenged with more miscarriages. Their road to parenthood has not been an easy one. They are seriously considering adoption. Whatever they choose, I know they will be wonderful parents.

My sisters and I and my husband, David, have frequently mused that one of us should write our mother's story. "Mom's story would make such a great soap opera." David went as far as buying a notebook and spending an afternoon writing a first chapter. Writing my story never crossed my mind or anyone else's. I had no idea when I began my research project ten years ago that the end result would be my story.

And yet now as I sit here finishing the last edits before sending the manuscript off to the publishers, it makes sense. What other story do any of us have but our own? I have been teaching clients and workshop participants this simple truth my entire professional life—own your own story.

We teach what we need to learn. And we teach it until we get it.

I finally got it. Now it is your turn. Go find your own story, claim it, appreciate it, don't deny it, and above all have compassion for it. In the end, what else do we have but our own story with all of its lessons and blessings?

Namaste,

Irene

Well that's it.
Thank you for taking the time to read my book. I hope you gained from the experience.

If you would like more information regarding my workshops and speaking engagements contact me at www.IreneTomkinson.com Let me know about you.

Blessings,
Irene

CPSIA information can be obtained at www.ICGtesting.com
Printed in the USA
LVOW06s1004060414

380507LV00002B/396/P